A/80/17

**General Assembly**
Official Records
Eighttieth Session
Supplement No. 17

# Report of the United Nations Commission on International Trade Law

## Fifty-eighth session
## (7–23 July 2025)



United Nations • New York, 2025

*Note*

Symbols of United Nations documents are composed of letters combined with figures. Mention of such a symbol indicates a reference to a United Nations document.

Print ISBN: 978-92-1-157784-6

Online ISBN: 978-92-1-1546941

# Contents

# I. Introduction

1. The present report of the United Nations Commission on International Trade Law (UNCITRAL) covers the fifty-eighth session of the Commission, held in Vienna from 7 to 23 July 2025.

2. Pursuant to General Assembly resolution 2205 (XXI) of 17 December 1966, the present report is submitted to the General Assembly and is also submitted for comments to the United Nations Conference on Trade and Development (UNCTAD).

# II. Organization of the session

## A. Opening of the session

3. The fifty-eighth session of the Commission was opened by the Under-Secretary-General for Legal Affairs and United Nations Legal Counsel, Ms. Elinor Hammarskjöld, on 7 July 2025.

## B. Membership and attendance

4. The General Assembly, in its resolution 2205 (XXI), established the Commission with a membership of 29 States, elected by the Assembly. By its resolution 3108 (XXVIII) of 12 December 1973, the General Assembly increased the membership of the Commission from 29 to 36 States. By its resolution 57/20 of 19 November 2002, the General Assembly further increased the membership of the Commission from 36 to 60 States. By its resolution 76/109 of 9 December 2021, the General Assembly increased the membership of the Commission from 60 to 70 States. Five of the additional 10 members were elected during the seventy-sixth session of the General Assembly, while the remaining five were to be elected during the seventy-ninth session of the Assembly.[1]

5. The current members of the Commission are the following States, whose term of office expires on the day prior to the beginning of the annual session of the Commission in the year indicated:[2] Afghanistan (2028), Argentina (2028), Armenia (2028), Australia (2028), Austria (2028), Belarus (2028), Belgium (2031), Bolivia (Plurinational State of) (2031), Brazil (2028), Bulgaria (2028), Burundi (2031), Canada (2031), Chile (2028), China (2031), Colombia (2028), Congo (2031), Côte d'Ivoire (2031), Czechia (2028), Democratic Republic of the Congo (2028), Dominican Republic (2031), El Salvador (2031), France (2031), Germany (2031), Ghana (2031), Greece (2028), Hungary (2031), India (2028), Iran (Islamic Republic of) (2028), Iraq (2028), Israel (2028), Italy (2028), Japan (2031), Kenya (2028), Kuwait (2028), Malawi (2028), Malaysia (2031), Mauritania (2031), Mauritius (2028), Mexico (2031), Morocco (2028), Netherlands (Kingdom of the) (2031), Nigeria (2028), Panama (2028), Peru (2031), Philippines (2031), Poland (2028), Republic of Korea (2031), Russian Federation (2031), Saudi Arabia (2028), Sierra Leone (2031), Singapore (2031), Somalia (2028), South Africa (2031), Spain (2028),

[1] As at 7 July 2025, three of the remaining five members had been elected, while two seats for the Group of Eastern European States remain vacant.

[2] Pursuant to General Assembly resolution 2205 (XXI), the members of the Commission are elected for a term of six years. Of the current membership, 34 were elected by the Assembly on 15 March 2022, at its seventy-sixth session, one was elected by the Assembly on 29 June 2022, at its seventy-sixth session, 31 were elected by the Assembly on 20 November 2024, at its seventy-ninth session, and two were elected by the Assembly on 16 June 2025, at its seventy-ninth session. By its resolution 31/99, the Assembly altered the dates of commencement and termination of membership by deciding that members would take office at the beginning of the first day of the regular annual session of the Commission immediately following their election and that their terms of office would expire on the day prior to the opening of the seventh regular annual session following their election.

Sri Lanka (2031), Sweden (2031), Switzerland (2031), Thailand (2028), Türkiye (2028), Turkmenistan (2028), Uganda (2028), Ukraine (2031), United Kingdom of Great Britain and Northern Ireland (2031), United States of America (2028), Uruguay (2031), Venezuela (Bolivarian Republic of) (2028), Viet Nam (2031) and Zambia (2031).

6. With the exception of Afghanistan, Bolivia (Plurinational State of), Burundi, the Congo, Malawi, Mauritius, Somalia, Sri Lanka and Zambia, all the members of the Commission were represented at the session.

7. The session was attended by observers from the following States: Algeria, Angola, Azerbaijan, Bahrain, Bosnia and Herzegovina, Burkina Faso, Cameroon, Chad, Costa Rica, Cuba, Denmark, Ecuador, Egypt, Finland, Guatemala, Honduras, Indonesia, Kazakhstan, Kyrgyzstan, Lao People's Democratic Republic, Libya, Liechtenstein, Lithuania, Madagascar, Malta, Myanmar, Namibia, Oman, Pakistan, Paraguay, Republic of Moldova, Serbia, Slovakia, United Arab Emirates, United Republic of Tanzania and Zimbabwe.

8. The session was also attended by observers from the State of Palestine and the European Union.

9. The session was further attended by observers from the following international organizations:

(a) United Nations system: World Bank Group;

(b) Intergovernmental organizations: Asian-African Legal Consultative Organization (AALCO), Commonwealth secretariat, Gulf Cooperation Council, Hague Conference on Private International Law (HCCH), International Institute for the Unification of Private Law (UNIDROIT), Organization of the Petroleum Exporting Countries and Permanent Court of Arbitration (PCA);

(c) Invited non-governmental organizations: Arab Planning Institute, ArbitralWomen, Asia Pacific Centre for Arbitration and Mediation, Asian Academy of International Law, Cairo Regional Centre for International Commercial Arbitration, Center for International Legal Studies, China Council for the Promotion of International Trade, China International Economic and Trade Arbitration Commission, China Society of Private International Law, Comité Maritime International, Conseil National des Administrateurs Judiciaires et Mandataires Judiciaires (France), Consumer Unity and Trust Society, European Blockchain Association, European Law Institute, European Law Students' Association, European Association of Restructuring and Insolvency Professionals (INSOL Europe), Global Shippers Forum, International and Comparative Law Research Center, International Bar Association, International Chamber of Commerce (ICC), International Chamber of Shipping, International Federation of Freight Forwarders Associations, International Group of Protection and Indemnity Clubs, International Law Institute, International Union of Notaries, National Association of Bankruptcy Trustees (United States of America), New York City Bar Association (United States of America), Organisation of Islamic Cooperation Arbitration Centre, Panel of Recognized International Market Experts in Finance, Shenzhen Court of International Arbitration (China), Stockholm Chamber of Commerce Arbitration Institute (Sweden), Tehran Chamber of Commerce, Industries, Mines and Agriculture (Islamic Republic of Iran), Ukrainian Arbitration Association and United States Council for International Business.

10. The Commission welcomed the participation of international non-governmental organizations with expertise in the major items on the agenda. The Commission noted that their participation was crucial for the quality of texts formulated by the Commission, and requested the secretariat to continue to invite such organizations to its sessions.

 

## C. Election of officers

11. The Commission elected the following officers:

*Chair*: Julia Emma Villatoro Tario (El Salvador)[3]

*Vice-Chairs*: Beate Czerwenka (Germany)
Xian Yong Harold Foo (Singapore)
Paul Kwabena Nana Sei Osei (Ghana)

*Rapporteur*: Meri Adamian (Armenia)

## D. Agenda

12. The agenda of the fifty-eighth session of the Commission as contained in document A/CN.9/1192 as adopted by the Commission at its 1234th meeting, on 7 July 2025, as follows:

1. Opening of the session.
2. Election of officers.
3. Adoption of the agenda.
4. Consideration of the draft convention on negotiable cargo documents.
5. Consideration of the draft model organization rules for limited liability enterprises.
6. Consideration of the draft toolkit and background notes on asset tracing and recovery in insolvency proceedings.
7. Consideration of the draft UNCITRAL-UNIDROIT study on the legal nature of verified carbon credits issued by independent carbon standard setters.
8. Consideration of the guidance document on legal issues relating to the use of distributed ledger technology in trade.
9. Consideration of the draft toolkit on dispute prevention and mitigation.
10. Progress reports of working groups.
11. Operationalization of the Advisory Centre on International Investment Dispute Resolution.
12. Work programme of the Commission:
    (a) Possible future work in the area of insolvency law;
    (b) Resource requirements to implement investor-State dispute settlement reform;
    (c) Climate change mitigation, adaptation and resilience;
    (d) Secured transactions using new types of assets and their treatment under the UNCITRAL Model Law on Secured Transactions (2016);
    (e) Dispute resolution in the digital economy;

[3] The UNCITRAL secretariat wishes to pay tribute to the Chair of the fifty-eighth session, who, despite facing serious health challenges, was steadfast in her commitment to chairing the session and sadly passed away shortly thereafter. Her dedication to the work of UNCITRAL is remembered with deep respect and appreciation. Although this tribute was not part of the report adopted by member States prior to the close of the session, the secretariat felt it appropriate, in compiling the report following the session, to include these lines in recognition of her dedication and in remembrance of her service.

(f) Electronic commerce and paperless trade;

(g) Other topics for future work;

(h) Working methods of UNCITRAL, including streamlining General Assembly omnibus resolutions.

13. Coordination and cooperation.

14. Non-legislative activities and other matters:

(a) Overview of non-legislative activities;

(b) Status and promotion of UNCITRAL legal texts;

(c) Relevant General Assembly resolutions;

(d) Current role of UNCITRAL in promoting the rule of law;

(e) Bibliography of recent writings related to the work of UNCITRAL.

15. Date and place of future meetings.

16. Other business:

(a) UNCITRAL at 60 celebrations;

(b) Other matters.

17. CLOUT Network meeting.

18. Adoption of the report of the Commission.

## E. Adoption of the report

13. The Commission adopted the present report by consensus at its 1253rd meeting, on 18 July 2025, at its 1257th meeting, on 22 July 2025, and at its 1258th meeting, on 23 July 2025.

# III. Summary of the work of the Commission at its fifty-eighth session

14. With respect to agenda item 4 (Consideration of the draft convention on negotiable cargo documents), the Commission approved the text of the draft convention, which is reproduced in annex I to the present report.

15. With respect to agenda item 5 (Consideration of the draft model organization rules for limited liability enterprises), the Commission endorsed both templates comprising the rules and authorized the secretariat to publish them as an annex to the *UNCITRAL Legislative Guide on Limited Liability Enterprises* (2021).[4]

16. With respect to agenda item 6 (Consideration of the draft toolkit and background notes on asset tracing and recovery in insolvency proceedings), the Commission adopted the draft texts under the title "Asset Tracing and Recovery in Insolvency Proceedings: UNCITRAL Toolkit and Background Notes".

17. With respect to agenda item 7 (Consideration of the draft UNCITRAL-UNIDROIT study on the legal nature of verified carbon credits issued by independent carbon standard setters), the Commission requested the secretariat to prepare a revised version of the study, which would reflect the relevant deliberations of the Commission at its current session, incorporate the technical comments received and include in an annex the policy-related comments received, and to make the revised version of the

[4] United Nations publication, Sales No. E.22.V.21.

study available on the website of the Commission in the six official languages of the United Nations, resources permitting.

18. With respect to agenda item 8 (Consideration of the guidance document on legal issues relating to the use of distributed ledger technology in trade), the Commission welcomed the draft guidance document and authorized the publication of the document in electronic form in the six official languages of the United Nations.

19. With respect to agenda item 9 (Consideration of the draft toolkit on dispute prevention and mitigation), the Commission adopted the UNCITRAL Toolkit on Prevention and Mitigation of International Investment Disputes.

20. With respect to agenda item 10 (Progress reports of working groups), the Commission took note of the progress report of Working Group II (Dispute Settlement), Working Group III (Investor-State Dispute Settlement Reform), Working Group IV (Electronic Commerce), Working Group V (Insolvency Law) and Working Group VI (Negotiable Cargo Documents). The Commission expressed its satisfaction with the progress made by those working groups.

21. With respect to agenda item 11 (Operationalization of the Advisory Centre on International Investment Dispute Resolution), the Commission agreed that the preparatory work should continue to be based on the Statute as adopted in principle, and that, on the basis of the outcome of the meetings on the operationalization of the Advisory Centre, it would aim to finalize the Statute at its fifty-ninth session, in 2026.

22. With respect to agenda item 12 (Work programme of the Commission), the Commission:

(a) Confirmed the programme of current legislative activities carried out by its Working Groups II, III, IV and V, and mandated Working Group VI to review the explanatory note on the draft convention on negotiable cargo documents;

(b) Authorized the secretariat to hold colloquiums on topics related to dispute resolution in the digital economy in conjunction with Working Group II sessions, and on possible future work in the area of insolvency law in conjunction with Working Group V sessions, and to utilize the conference resources tentatively allocated to Working Group I in the second half of 2025 and the first half of 2026, as well as any conference resources of other working groups that may become available, to hold colloquiums on secured transactions, end-to-end trade digitalization, paperless trade, digital platforms and digital payments (see subparagraph (e) below);

(c) Requested the secretariat to conduct preparatory work, in coordination with relevant international organizations, to refine the scope of possible work on updating the UNCITRAL Model Law on Public Procurement (2011) and related texts to reflect recent developments, which would not include issues pertaining to climate change mitigation, adaptation and resilience;

(d) Instructed the secretariat to continue to monitor developments related to secured transactions using new types of assets, and to convene an expert group meeting or a colloquium involving representatives of relevant international organizations to define the scope and form of any future work in that area;

(e) In respect of topics related to digital trade:

(i) Requested the secretariat to continue its exploratory work on the project on dispute resolution in the digital economy, including by circulating a questionnaire to States for input;

(ii) Requested the secretariat to continue its preparatory work on enabling end-to-end trade digitalization and paperless trade, including by holding a colloquium to explore the use of UNCITRAL texts on electronic commerce for paperless trade;

(iii) Requested the secretariat to monitor developments on legal issues relating to the use of decentralized autonomous organizations in trade and to carry out further exploratory work on those issues, including in cooperation with HCCH;

(iv) Requested the secretariat to conduct exploratory work on legal aspects of digital trade with a focus on digital platforms and private law, including an assessment of the desirability and feasibility of developing a harmonized legal text, possibly in the form of a model law;

(v) Requested the secretariat to carry out exploratory work on the topic of digital payments, carefully considering any intersection of that work with existing regulatory frameworks;

(f) In respect of its working methods:

(i) Requested the secretariat to compile possible cost-saving and efficiency-enhancing measures proposed during the current session and analyse the budget savings and their implications for the functioning of the Commission, the working groups and the secretariat, and to facilitate intersessional consultations on means of enhancing the efficiency of the Commission;

(ii) Agreed to recommend to the General Assembly that it grant the Commission the necessary resources to allow the livestreaming of Commission and working group sessions;

(iii) Recommended that the project proposal template proposed during the current session be communicated to member States for their consideration and be made available on the website of the Commission;

(g) Decided to recommend to the General Assembly that additional conference time and supporting resources be allocated to the secretariat for a period of two more years, from 2026 to 2027, in order to continue with the investor-State dispute settlement reform project outlined in document A/CN.9/1217.

23. Also with respect to agenda item 12, under the sub-item "Working methods of UNCITRAL, including streamlining General Assembly omnibus resolutions", the Commission requested that the outcome of the intersessional consultative process aimed at streamlining General Assembly resolutions on UNCITRAL annual reports be communicated by the secretariat to States Members of the United Nations through their permanent missions in Vienna.

24. With respect to agenda item 13 (Coordination and cooperation), the Commission took note of the reports by the Secretariat on coordination activities and on international governmental and non-governmental organizations invited to sessions of UNCITRAL and its working groups, as well as the reports by AALCO, the Commonwealth secretariat, HCCH, ICC, the International Organisation of La Francophonie, PCA, UNIDROIT, the Center for International Legal Studies and the China Society of Private International Law.

25. With respect to agenda item 14 (Non-legislative activities and other matters), the Commission took note of the reports by the Secretariat concerning non-legislative activities and other matters. More specifically:

(a) The Commission expressed appreciation to its secretariat for the non-legislative activities carried out in 2024 (including the increased promotional activities related to the transparency repository and the UNCITRAL transparency standards) and the holistic and interdisciplinary approach taken to those activities. The Commission also expressed appreciation to:

(i) The Republic of Korea and Hong Kong, China, for their continued contributions to the operation of the UNCITRAL Regional Centre for Asia and the Pacific;

(ii) Japan for its financial contribution to the project on dispute resolution in the digital economy and its forthcoming contribution of a legal expert, as announced during the current session, to support the programme activities of the UNCITRAL Regional Centre for Asia and the Pacific;

(iii) The European Union and the Federal Ministry for Economic Cooperation and Development of Germany for providing funding that would make it possible for the Secretary-General to continue to operate the transparency repository, through the secretariat of the Commission, until the end of 2027;

(iv) China, Saudi Arabia, the International Training Centre of the International Labour Organization and the European Bank for Reconstruction and Development for their contribution to and support for the development of the UNCITRAL e-learning programme;

(v) Switzerland for its forthcoming contribution, as announced during the current session, to support the implementation of investor-State dispute settlement reforms;

(vi) The General Assembly for its support in furthering the dissemination of UNCITRAL texts;

(b) The Commission appealed to:

(i) Governments, the relevant bodies of the United Nations system, organizations, institutions and individuals to make voluntary contributions to the trust fund for UNCITRAL symposiums and the trust fund established to provide travel assistance to developing countries that are members of the Commission; to finance special projects; and to otherwise assist the secretariat in carrying out non-legislative activities;

(ii) Relevant stakeholders to provide additional resources and other support to the UNCITRAL Regional Centre for Asia and the Pacific;

(iii) All interested States, organizations, institutions and individuals to consider making contributions to the trust fund for UNCITRAL symposiums earmarked for the purposes of upgrading the Case Law on UNCITRAL Texts (CLOUT) database and translating courses in the UNCITRAL e-learning programme into the six official languages of the United Nations;

(iv) Publishers, especially those representing or affiliated with organizations invited to UNCITRAL sessions, to donate their UNCITRAL-related books, periodicals and other materials to the UNCITRAL Law Library, or grant a discounted rate for such materials;

(c) The Commission encouraged the secretariat to continue to explore and expand the online presence of UNCITRAL as appropriate, resources permitting. The Commission further encouraged efforts by all concerned to ensure equitable representation, inclusivity, multilingualism and other objectives of the United Nations internship programme in the internship programme of the UNCITRAL secretariat.

26. With respect to agenda item 15 (Date and place of future meetings), the Commission approved the holding of its fifty-ninth session in New York from 22 June to 10 July 2026 and the schedule for working group sessions (including colloquiums) in the second half of 2025 and in 2026.

27. With respect to agenda item 16 (Other business), the Commission called upon Governments and relevant stakeholders to host or support activities to celebrate the significant milestone of the Commission's sixtieth anniversary and to further strengthen UNCITRAL and its work.

28. With respect to agenda item 17 (CLOUT Network meeting), the Commission renewed its strong support for the CLOUT system and took note of various suggestions aimed at enhancing the system and increasing its visibility.

# IV. Finalization and approval of the draft convention on negotiable cargo documents

## A. Introduction

29. The Commission recalled the decision made at its fifty-fifth session, in 2022, to assign the topic of negotiable multimodal transport documents to Working Group VI,[5] which had subsequently considered that topic over six sessions, from its forty-first to its forty-sixth sessions. At its fifty-sixth session, in 2023, the Commission had expressed its satisfaction with the progress made by the Working Group.[6] At its fifty-seventh session, in 2024, the Commission had been informed that significant progress had been made on the draft instrument on negotiable cargo documents and that the Working Group might be in a position to transmit the draft instrument to the Commission for review and possible adoption at the Commission's next session, in 2025.[7]

30. At the current session, the Commission had before it the reports of Working Group VI on the work of its forty-fifth and forty-sixth sessions (A/CN.9/1199 and A/CN.9/1205). It also had before it the text of the draft convention on negotiable cargo documents (A/CN.9/1213), a compilation of comments submitted by States and relevant international organizations on the draft convention (A/CN.9/1214 and A/CN.9/1214/Add.1), and a note by the Secretariat on the interaction between the draft convention on negotiable cargo documents and existing international transport law conventions as presented to the Working Group at its forty-sixth session (A/CN.9/WG.VI/WP.115).

31. The following paragraphs summarize the deliberations of the Commission and the amendments to the draft convention that were agreed upon. Provisions of the draft convention not referred to below were approved by the Commission as they appear in document A/CN.9/1213, subject to stylistic and linguistic adjustments that the secretariat was requested to make to ensure consistency in the text of the convention and conformity with United Nations editorial guidelines and official style.

## B. Consideration of the draft convention

32. The Commission proceeded to consider the draft convention article by article.

### 1. Article 1. Scope of application

#### (a) Paragraph 1

33. The Commission heard the following proposals regarding the connecting factors listed in paragraph 1 (a) and (b):

(a) A proposal to replace the words "as provided for in the transport contract" with "as indicated in the negotiable cargo document" in subparagraphs (a) and (b) received broad support, although a query was raised about the logic of defining the scope of application of the convention by reference to the contents of the very document that it created. With regard to subparagraph (b), it was observed that the content-related requirement for the place of delivery of the goods to be indicated in a negotiable cargo document under article 4, paragraph 1 (h), was not strictly mandatory given that, pursuant to article 5, paragraph 1, an omission of such information would not affect the validity of the negotiable cargo document;

[5] *Official Records of the General Assembly, Seventy-seventh Session, Supplement No. 17* (A/77/17), para. 202. At the fifty-sixth session, the title of the Working Group was changed to "Negotiable Cargo Documents" to clarify that its work covered both multimodal and unimodal transport contexts (ibid., *Seventy-eighth Session, Supplement No. 17* (A/78/17), para. 174 (f)).

[6] Ibid., *Seventy-eighth Session, Supplement No. 17* (A/78/17), para. 171.

[7] Ibid., *Seventy-ninth Session, Supplement No. 17* (A/79/17), para. 261.

(b) A proposal to refer to the actual place of taking in charge and delivery of the goods, rather than the place indicated in the negotiable cargo document, did not receive support. It was observed that the eventual place of delivery might not be the place indicated in the negotiable cargo document, and that referring to the actual place of delivery could create legal uncertainty. It was added that, by referring to what was indicated in the negotiable cargo document, subparagraph (b) did not preclude the common practice of changing the place of delivery during transit, and that such a change would not affect the application of the convention or indeed the effect or validity of the negotiable cargo document;

(c) A proposal to replace "or" with "and" in subparagraph (a), such that the connecting factors applied cumulatively, did not receive support. The Commission was referred to earlier deliberations within the Working Group on the issue (A/CN.9/1164, para. 16), and the desirability of ensuring broader scope of application was reiterated.

34. The Commission heard the following proposals for additional connecting factors, those proposals being based on suggestions already put forward within the Working Group (A/CN.9/1205, para. 22):

(a) One proposal was for the convention to apply where the negotiable cargo document was issued in a State Party. While uncertainty had been expressed within the Working Group about how to identify the place of issuance of an electronic negotiable cargo document, it was clarified that the proposed connecting factor was concerned with the place of issuance "as indicated in the negotiable cargo document", which was already a mandatory content requirement under article 4. Broad support was expressed for that proposal;

(b) Another proposal, which received some support, was for the convention to apply where the rules of private international law led to the application of the law of a State Party. It was observed that a similar connecting factor was contained in other conventions prepared by UNCITRAL, notably the United Nations Convention on Contracts for the International Sale of Goods (1980)[8] and the United Nations Convention on the Carriage of Goods by Sea (1978)[9] (the "Hamburg Rules"), and that such a connecting factor would be reasonable given that the convention was intended to ensure party autonomy. In response, it was pointed out that the connecting factor in those other conventions was concerned with the law applicable to the underlying contract (the contract of sale and the contract of carriage, respectively), which was governed by the convention concerned, whereas in the convention, which did not govern the underlying transport contract, the connecting factor would be concerned with the law applicable to the negotiable cargo documents as a document of title. It was added that legal systems differed significantly with respect to their rules of private international law applicable to documents of title, and that the proposed connecting factor would create legal uncertainty.

35. After discussion, the Commission agreed to retain the chapeau of the paragraph as drafted and to replace subparagraphs (a) and (b) with the following:

"(a) The place of taking in charge of the goods by the transport operator as indicated in the negotiable cargo document is located in a State Party;

"(b) The place of delivery of the goods by the transport operator as indicated in the negotiable cargo document is located in a State Party; or

"(c) The place of issuance of the negotiable cargo document as indicated in the negotiable cargo document is located in a State Party."

[8] United Nations, *Treaty Series*, vol. 1489, No. 25567, p. 3.

[9] United Nations, *Treaty Series*, vol. 1695, No. 29215, p. 3.

### (b) Paragraph 2

36. The Commission agreed to retain paragraph 2 as drafted. Requirements for customs clearance were cited as an example of the types of laws covered by the paragraph.

### (c) Paragraph 3

37. The Commission heard a proposal to amend the paragraph by deleting the words "except as otherwise provided for herein". Concerns were expressed as to the effect of the paragraph as a supremacy clause. It was observed that, if the convention did not concern the creation of new substantive rights and obligations, the words were superfluous and the issue of incompatibility with other treaties, as addressed in article 30 of the Vienna Convention on the Law of Treaties,[10] did not arise. In response, it was observed that, even if the convention did not seek to modify the rights established under the transport contract, it did affect the exercise of those rights insofar as they were incorporated into the negotiable cargo document and transferred to the holder of the negotiable cargo document under article 7. Reference was made to a similar observation made by the Working Group (A/CN.9/1164, para. 91). Reference was also made to article 8 concerning the procedure whereby the transport operator should seek missing information, instructions or documents. Accordingly, it was said that the words were operative and should be retained. Support was expressed for that view. It was also highlighted that the paragraph was intended to give the convention precedence over conventions relating to the carriage of goods by road or rail, which did not provide for negotiable transport documents.

38. Another proposal to specify that the issuance and use of a negotiable cargo document under the convention, rather than the convention itself, did not modify rights and obligations was not taken up.

39. A proposal to insert the words "for any mode of transport" at the end of the paragraph was also not taken up. It was noted that a lack of clear and uniform rules on documents of title representing goods in transit created challenges when trade finance was sought, as it required banks to assess the laws of different countries.

### (d) Application of the convention to transport involving a maritime leg

40. The Commission was referred to the several suggestions contained in the comments submitted by States and international organizations to limit the application of the convention in respect of the transport of goods involving a maritime leg, mostly under chapter 5, concerning final clauses.

41. The Commission discussed at length a proposal to insert a new paragraph in article 1 along the following lines:

> "This Convention shall not apply in respect of any transport document issued pursuant to a transport contract that provides for carriage by sea or to which any international convention or national law on the carriage of goods wholly or partly by sea applies."

42. In support of the proposal, it was pointed out that there was a risk of overlap between the convention on negotiable cargo documents and pre-existing conventions dealing with contracts for the carriage of goods by sea and bills of lading, especially those issued as negotiable documents. It was emphasized that the convention should not interfere with well-established rules governing bills of lading. It was noted that the scope of application of the convention should be limited to the original objective of the project, which was to introduce negotiability in modes of transport where negotiability was not practised, namely land-based transport. The inclusion of maritime transport within the scope of the convention might require States to make substantial revisions to their laws on the carriage of goods by sea, and could face

[10] United Nations, *Treaty Series*, vol. 1155, No. 18232, p. 331.

strong opposition from States. It was questioned whether a negotiable cargo document would be considered as a document of title similar to a bill of lading under the International Convention for the Unification of Certain Rules of Law Relating to Bills of Lading (the "Hague Rules"), thereby triggering the application of rules thereunder regarding substantive rights and obligations on which the parties might wish to rely. While the "opt in" nature of the convention was emphasized, whereby a negotiable cargo document was only issued if agreed between the transport operator and the consignor, it was noted that other parties (for instance, maritime carriers and banks) might still be affected by the consequences of issuing a negotiable cargo document.

43. The Commission recalled that applying the convention to maritime transport had been extensively discussed within the Working Group (A/CN.9/1205, paras. 13–17), where strong support had been expressed for not limiting its scope of application. It was noted that the body of legal rules governing maritime bills of lading were not unified and that differences existed in the sources of rights under a maritime bill of lading among different jurisdictions. It was added that uncertainty existed as to the legal nature of maritime bills of lading, including with regard to the nature of "title" in the goods, and whether the holder had a direct right to sue the carrier to the exclusion of the consignor. It was also pointed out that only some jurisdictions had enacted a dedicated bill of lading law that existed alongside existing maritime law conventions, and that changes to such laws had not affected the application of those conventions. It was stressed that no concrete examples of conflict between the Hague Rules and the draft convention had been identified, which was a necessary precondition for entertaining a proposal to limit the convention's scope. It was emphasized that the legal characterization of transport documents issued for multimodal transport involving a maritime leg remained unclear under international conventions and national law. In any event, the Commission was cautioned against excluding such documents entirely from the scope of the convention given that a significant portion of international trade involved maritime transport in whole or in part. In that regard, it was observed that the proposed new paragraph covered not only unimodal maritime transport but also multimodal transport involving a maritime leg. It was suggested that only unimodal maritime transport should be excluded, which could be achieved by not including the words "or partly" in the proposed new paragraph.

44. With regard to the original objective of the project, it was observed that the intention had always been to develop a uniform and consistent legal framework for the use of negotiable documents of title for both multimodal and unimodal international shipments and that maritime transport had not been excluded from the scope at the outset. The longstanding practice of freight forwarders acting as contractual carriers and issuing multimodal bills of lading was highlighted as a practice that had not created any difficulties regarding the application of existing maritime law conventions. It was added that, given the convention's "opt in" nature, its application to all modes of transport would enable freight forwarders, shippers and banks to organize multimodal end-to-end or unimodal transportation as the circumstances required. As the convention could facilitate trade and market access in complex global supply chains, it was also observed that States should not be deprived of the benefits of the convention. It was added that the maritime industry could also benefit from innovations that the convention offered. Concern was expressed that excluding maritime transport from the scope of application of the convention would defeat the key objective of developing a single negotiable cargo document covering the multimodal transport of goods. Furthermore, such exclusion would reduce the impact of the convention on economic development, particularly for coastal developing States.

45. After discussion, the Commission decided not to limit the scope of application of the convention in article 1. It was acknowledged that that decision did not preclude the consideration of other possible mechanisms affecting scope, such as limiting the circumstances in which a negotiable cargo document could be issued under article 3 or allowing States to make reservations.

### 2. Article 2. Definitions

#### (a) "Consignor"

46. The Commission agreed to retain the definition of "consignor" as drafted.

#### (b) "Consignee"

47. While the following proposals were made to amend the definition of "consignee", the Commission agreed to retain it as drafted:

(a) One proposal was to refer to the person entitled to take delivery of the goods "under the transport contract" as opposed to the person "named in the transport contract". Although it was acknowledged that that proposal reflected the fact that the convention was not concerned with the contents of the transport contract, it was noted that the proposed wording could pose additional challenges;

(b) Another proposal was to delete the definition entirely. It was noted that the term "consignee" was used only in article 1, paragraph 3, and article 4, paragraph 1 (j), and that, in the latter provision, the term "holder" should be used instead. In response, it was noted that it was helpful to define the four major roles recognized in the convention, namely the transport operator, consignor, consignee and holder, regardless of the frequency of their use.

#### (c) "Electronic record"

48. The Commission agreed to retain the definition of "electronic record" as drafted and to remove the square brackets.

49. A query was raised as to whether the reference to information "logically associated" with the record could be interpreted as encompassing paper documents. In response, it was recalled that the definition had been taken from the UNCITRAL Model Law on Electronic Transferable Records (2017),[11] and the desirability of maintaining consistency in terminology was reiterated. Attention was drawn to the statement in the explanatory note to the Model Law that "logically" referred to computer software and not to human logic. The definition reflected the recognition that data comprising an electronic negotiable cargo document would change throughout the document's life cycle, including when it was endorsed. It was noted that the meaning of the definition could be elaborated on in the explanatory note on the convention.

#### (d) "Holder"

50. The Commission agreed to retain the definition of "holder" as drafted.

51. A proposal to delete the reference to "a blank endorsed order document" was not taken up. It was recalled that the issue had been considered by the Working Group, in which it had been noted that blank endorsed documents were fairly common in practice (A/CN.9/1199, para. 54).

#### (e) "Negotiable cargo document"

52. The Commission agreed to retain the definition of "negotiable cargo document" as drafted.

53. A proposal to replace the words "consigned to the order of the holder" with "consigned to the holder" was not taken up, since national legal systems differed as to the characterization of a document endorsed blank as an order document. Proposals to include a requirement in the definition to indicate the number of originals and to refer to goods being "delivered" to the holder did not receive support. Concerns were

[11] *Official Records of the General Assembly, Seventy-second Session, Supplement No. 17* (A/72/17), annex I.

reiterated about linking the validity of a negotiable cargo document with the requirement to indicate the number of originals (A/CN.9/1164, para. 72).

### (f) Other definitions

54. While a suggestion was made to merge the definitions of "transport contract", "transport document" and "transport operator" into a single provision, it was noted that there was value in maintaining separate definitions for each term. The Commission also heard the following proposals to align the definitions, none of which were taken up:

(a) Several proposals sought to require parity of parties as between the transport contract and the transport document. One proposal was to amend the chapeau of article 2, paragraph 7, which set out the definition of "transport document", to refer to a document issued by the transport operator. In response, it was observed that such an amendment would effectively exclude consignment notes issued by the consignor. Another proposal was to amend article 2, paragraph 7 (a), to specify that the transport document evidenced or contained the transport contract "between the transport operator and the consignor". In response, it was noted that the definitions of "transport contract" and "transport operator" sufficiently clarified that the parties to the transport contract would be the same as the parties to the transport document;

(b) It was observed that the definition of "transport contract" referred to the transport operator undertaking to perform transport of the goods, while the definition of "transport operator" referred to that party assuming responsibility for the performance of the contract. A proposal was made to align the two definitions. While some support was expressed for the proposal, it was observed that the reference to "responsibility" was important for ensuring that the convention accommodated the issuance of a negotiable cargo document by a freight forwarder acting as a contractual carrier without performing the carriage itself (A/CN.9/1134, para. 52).

## 3. Article 3. Issuance of a negotiable cargo document

### (a) Paragraph 1

55. The Commission agreed to replace the words "a conspicuous annotation with reference to this Convention" with "a conspicuous reference to this Convention" on the basis that the term "annotation" should be used only to refer to information entered into a transport document to "upgrade" it to a negotiable cargo document. It was noted that the same change would need to be made in article 1, paragraph 1.

56. The importance of the word "conspicuous" and the need to ensure that the reference to the convention was not hidden among the general conditions applicable to the transport document were emphasized (A/CN.9/1164, paras. 29 and 32). It was added that the meaning of the term "conspicuous" should be elaborated on in the explanatory note.

57. Another proposal to require a negotiable cargo document to expressly indicate that it was issued subject to the convention on negotiable cargo documents did not receive support.

### (b) Paragraph 2

58. It was observed that paragraph 2 provided a non-exhaustive list of methods for issuing a negotiable cargo document. While it was acknowledged that prescribing how negotiable cargo documents could be issued, particularly the circumstances for their issuance as a separate document, could help reduce legal uncertainty, concerns were expressed that such a change would remove the requirement for the transport operator and the consignor to agree on the method of issuance; therefore, the Commission expressed support for retaining the chapeau as drafted to maintain flexibility.

59. The Commission agreed to delete the words in square brackets in subparagraph (a) on the basis that a transport operator should be allowed to insert missing mandatory content by entering the annotation. However, a view was expressed that the words could help eliminate the need to amend transport documents governed by other transport law conventions. The Commission also agreed to require the annotation to be entered in "each original of the transport document".

60. It was explained that the requirement for the annotation to be signed was aimed at ensuring that the transport operator was responsible for the annotation rather than – as might be the case with regard to consignment notes issued under some existing transport conventions – the consignor. It was added that that understanding should be reflected in the explanatory note, which should also explain the interaction between that requirement and the requirement to sign the negotiable cargo document itself.

#### (c) Paragraph 3

61. The Commission agreed that paragraph 3 should require that the annotation contain the indication set out in article 2, paragraph 5, or wording to that effect. Although it was implicit that that requirement must be fulfilled in order for a negotiable cargo document within the meaning of the convention to be issued, a strong preference was expressed for a more explicit reference to the content requirements forming part of that definition.

62. The Commission agreed to delete subparagraph (b) on the basis that it was unnecessary.

#### (d) Paragraph 4

63. It was explained that the second sentence of paragraph 4 was concerned with the issuance of negotiable cargo documents after the goods were taken in charge rather than the method of issuing the negotiable cargo document, which was addressed in paragraph 2. Accordingly, it was agreed to amend the second sentence as follows: "If so agreed between the transport operator and the consignor, the transport operator may issue a negotiable cargo document at a later stage where a transport document has been issued" and to delete the two subparagraphs. It was suggested that the interaction between paragraphs 2 and 4 could be elaborated on in the explanatory note.

64. The Commission also agreed that the words "subject to paragraph 1" in the first sentence were redundant and should be deleted.

#### (e) Paragraph 5

65. The Commission did not take up a proposal to clarify the meaning of the term "negotiable transport document", which was generally understood and covered maritime bills of lading. It was explained that the paragraph was designed to safeguard against the issuance of multiple negotiable documents in respect of the same goods and thus multiple competing claims. Reference was made to the practice by freight forwarders of issuing a multimodal bill of lading and subsequently requesting the issuance of a non-negotiable straight bill of lading from a maritime carrier. It was suggested that the explanatory note should clarify that the paragraph was not intended to prohibit the issuance of a straight bill of lading after the issuance of a negotiable cargo document in a multimodal context.

### 4. Article 4. Contents of the negotiable cargo document

#### (a) Paragraph 1

66. The Commission revisited the suggestion to amend subparagraph (j) (see para. 47 above). After further discussion, broad support emerged for replacing the reference to "consignee" with a more general reference to freight being payable "at destination".

67. Broad support was expressed for removing mandatory content requirements that applied when the negotiable cargo document was "issued separately". However, support was also expressed for inserting a requirement that a stand-alone negotiable cargo document make reference to the transport contract. It was observed that the provisions applicable to stand-alone negotiable cargo documents in the draft convention did not require an express link with the transport contract, and that such a link should be ensured.

68. After discussion, the Commission agreed to replace subparagraphs (f) and (g) with the following:

"(f) The place and date of issuance of the negotiable cargo document;

(g) If issued as a stand-alone negotiable cargo document, a reference to the transport contract;"

69. In its consideration of article 7, the Commission revisited the requirement in subparagraph (g) (see para. 82 below).

### (b) Paragraph 2

70. The Commission did not take up a proposal to delete the proviso "if expressly agreed upon between the consignor and the transport operator" in subparagraph (a). It was noted that the proviso acknowledged that, in practice, it was not uncommon for the timetable for delivery to remain unsettled at the time of issuance of the negotiable cargo document. The Commission did, however, take up a proposal to delete the proviso "if known at the time of issuance of the negotiable cargo document" in subparagraph (b) on the basis that the information listed therein could only be included if it was known at the time of issuance, and that in any case paragraph 2 listed non-mandatory items of information.

71. The Commission did not take up a proposal to include the name of the ship as an additional item. It was observed that such information was typically not known at the time of shipment and could in any event be included under subparagraph (d). It was queried whether the convention should single out a means of transport that was specific to one mode of transport.

### 5. Article 5. Deficiencies in the negotiable cargo document

72. Recalling its decision to remove the references in article 4 to negotiable cargo documents "issued separately" (see para. 67 above), the Commission agreed to delete the second sentence of article 5, paragraph 3. It was noted that, while article 3, paragraph 2, permitted the issuance of a negotiable cargo document in addition to a transport document, that method of issuance could pose difficulties and should not be expressly contemplated in the convention.

73. The Commission agreed to retain the remaining part of article 5 as drafted.

### 6. Article 6. Evidentiary effect of the negotiable cargo document

74. A proposal was made to require the transport operator to specify in the negotiable cargo document the grounds for qualifying any information under paragraph 1. Some support was expressed for the proposal, which reflected a similar requirement contained in article 16, paragraph 1, of the Hamburg Rules. However, it was pointed out that such a requirement could raise additional questions, such as the level of detail required for compliance and the legal consequences of non-compliance. It was added that subparagraphs (a) and (b) of that paragraph already prescribed the grounds for the transport operator to qualify information furnished by the consignor and that, if anything, the need to specify the grounds for such qualification could be addressed by indicating in the negotiable cargo document which subparagraph a qualification was made under.

75. The Commission did not take up the proposal but instead suggested that the explanatory note should provide guidance on that issue. The Commission agreed to retain article 6 as drafted.

### 7. Article 7. Rights of the holder under a negotiable cargo document

76. The Commission agreed to amend the heading of the article to read: "Rights of the holder of a negotiable cargo document".

#### (a) Paragraph 1

77. It was explained that paragraph 1 was concerned with the rights acquired by a holder other than the consignor. Noting that the "first" holder of a negotiable cargo document might not necessarily be the consignor, it was observed that such a holder would not be covered if paragraph 1 applied only to a person who became a holder pursuant to article 11. Broad support was expressed for clarifying the application of paragraph 1 by referring to a "holder that is not the consignor" rather than a "person who becomes a holder of a negotiable cargo document pursuant to article 11".

78. It was noted that, despite its heading, article 7 did not clearly address the rights of the consignor as the holder of the negotiable cargo document. The Commission was invited to consider including a provision to that effect.

79. The concern was expressed that the concept of rights being "incorporated" into a negotiable cargo document was open to interpretation. It was added that a rule providing for the holder to acquire the rights incorporated in the negotiable cargo document was too limitative as it would deprive the holder of rights that it might otherwise enjoy as the holder of, for example, a maritime bill of lading under applicable law, including the benefits that it might enjoy under any mandatory provisions, such as restrictions on limiting liability under the transport contract.

80. To address those concerns, a proposal was made to delete the words "to the extent that these rights are incorporated in the negotiable cargo document". The insertion of a reference to rights provided for in the law applicable to the transport contract was also proposed. It was stressed that the deletion was intended to put the holder in a more favourable position and that it did not depart from the principle that the holder should be able to rely exclusively on the information in the negotiable cargo document (see A/CN.9/1205, para. 33). It was observed that, in practice, the types of transport documents that could be "upgraded" to a negotiable cargo document would contain the terms of the transport contract, and that that could be complemented by a requirement for stand-alone negotiable cargo documents to contain the terms of the transport contract. It was added that, in case of conflict between the transport contract and information in the negotiable cargo document, the latter would prevail under article 6, paragraph 3, and article 7, paragraph 2.

81. The following arguments were presented in response to that proposal:

(a) Firstly, it was observed that the concept of rights being "incorporated" into a document of title was sufficiently clear, the concept being used in other international instruments and its meaning having been elaborated on within the Working Group (A/CN.9/1205, para. 62). A view was expressed that incorporating rights under the transport contract did not mean that the transport contract was subsumed under the negotiable cargo document; the former would continue to exist separately. Accordingly, a consignor who was not the holder of the negotiable cargo document could still rely on the transport contract to exercise its rights, other than those incorporated in the negotiable cargo document;

(b) Secondly, it was emphasized that the wording in paragraph 1 represented a compromise reached within the Working Group after extensive deliberation, as well as a compromise between approaches taken by different legal systems as to the nature of the rights held by a person by virtue of becoming the holder;

(c) Thirdly, it was observed that the proposal effectively reverted to a position that the Working Group had considered and rejected early on in its work, and that it represented a fundamental change to the understanding that had emerged within the Working Group that the negotiable cargo document alone should determine the rights of the holder, which should not need to rely on the transport contract to exercise its rights;

(d) Fourthly, the proposal would introduce an approach inconsistent with the current practice of maritime bills of lading and would limit efforts to standardize negotiable cargo documents, thereby reducing the benefits that the convention could offer and diminishing its appeal to potential users.

82. It was suggested that some of the concerns regarding the proposal could be addressed by requiring the negotiable cargo document to contain not only a reference to the transport contract but also the terms of that contract. Recalling its earlier deliberations (see paras. 67 and 68 above), the Commission agreed to further amend article 4, paragraph 1 (g), on the basis of the suggestion.

83. It was noted that referring to the rights under the transport contract might imply that the holder should have reviewed the transport contract, which could impose an unreasonable burden on the holder (for example, where the holder was a bank). It was also pointed out that referring to rights under applicable law imposed an additional burden, as holders would need to conduct a full assessment of that law. In response, it was suggested that the explanatory note should clarify that a holder was under no duty to check information in the transport contract or to conduct an assessment of the applicable law.

84. The view was also expressed that referring to applicable law would be stating the obvious, as the rights of the holder would in any event be subject to the law applicable to the transport contract.

85. Support was expressed for retaining the list of rights in paragraph 1 as an illustrative list.

86. After discussion, the Commission agreed to revise the chapeau of paragraph 1 as follows, and to retain the rest of the paragraph as drafted: "A person other than the consignor who becomes a holder of a negotiable cargo document shall, by virtue of becoming the holder, have acquired the rights under the transport contract, including those provided for in the law applicable to the transport contract. Such rights may include:". The Commission revisited the drafting of paragraph 1 in subsequent deliberations (see paras. 90–92 below).

### (b) Paragraph 2

87. To reflect the application of paragraph 1 as clarified within the Commission (see para. 77 above), it was agreed to replace the words "a holder under article 11" in paragraph 2 with "a holder that is not the consignor", which was the formulation used in article 9. The Commission agreed to retain the rest of the paragraph as drafted.

### (c) Paragraph 3

88. It was suggested that relocating paragraph 3 to the beginning of article 7 could alleviate the concern expressed regarding article 7 as revised. It was proposed to reformulate the paragraph in its new location as follows:

> "Upon the issuance of a negotiable cargo document, any entitlement to the rights provided for in the negotiable cargo document can only be exercised by the holder, which shall include the right to demand delivery of the goods at destination."

89. It was explained that the reformulated paragraph served not only to deny (to a person other than the holder) but also to award (to the holder) the entitlement to exercise rights. It was added that the concept of rights being "provided for" in the

negotiable cargo document was clearer than that of their being "incorporated in" the document and allowed greater flexibility than the concept of rights being "stated" in the document. It was also clarified that the additional phrase at the end of the reformulated paragraph was intended to ensure that, regardless of the actual contents of the negotiable cargo document, the holder had the right to demand delivery (as set out in current article 7, paragraph 1 (a)).

90. A proposal was also made to further revise current paragraph 1 as follows:

> "A person other than the consignor who becomes a holder of a negotiable cargo document shall, by virtue of becoming the holder, have acquired the right to bring a claim against the transport operator and the right of disposal (as applicable) under the transport contract, as well as those rights provided for in the law applicable to the transport contract, as if it were a party to that contract."

91. It was explained that (a) the paragraph would apply in addition to the reformulated and relocated paragraph 3; (b) the words "as applicable" would indicate that the right of disposal would only be acquired if it existed under the transport contract; and (c) the rights provided for in the law applicable to the transport contract would have been acquired additionally. A view was expressed that the right to demand delivery would encompass a claim for delayed delivery.

92. After discussion, the Commission agreed to both proposals and to renumber current paragraphs 1 and 2 accordingly.

**(d) Paragraph 4**

93. It was noted that paragraph 4 was a key provision that sought to bridge differences between legal systems as to the nature of rights that the holder acquired in respect of the goods. It was suggested that the issue could be elaborated on further in the explanatory note.

**(e) Paragraph 5**

94. The Commission agreed to update the cross reference to the right of disposal.

**8. Article 8. Missing information, instructions or documents**

95. A view was expressed that article 8 was unbalanced in favour of the holder and imposed an unreasonable burden on the transport operator. It was emphasized that the transport operator should not be expected to seek information or instructions from a holder if the holder was unknown to it. It was also noted that it would be difficult to assess whether a transport operator had made reasonable efforts to obtain such information or instructions, and that the convention did not specify the legal consequences for failing to do so. The Commission heard a proposal to clarify that the transport operator would only need to seek information or instructions from a holder that was known to it, as well as a proposal to delete the provision altogether.

96. The Commission was reminded of the importance of the provision, as the carrier might need instructions to carry out the contract or deliver the goods and should, for that purpose, be able to seek instructions from the party in control of the goods, namely the negotiable cargo document holder (A/CN.9/1127, para. 87). It was reiterated that obliging the holder to provide information requested by the transport operator should be avoided on the basis that banks might not be in a position to provide such information (A/CN.9/1127, para. 88; A/CN.9/1170, para. 11). It was explained that the second sentence of article 8 provided that the transport operator should proceed in accordance with the transport contract if the transport operator was not able to contact the holder after reasonable effort. A suggestion was made to refer to a specific time frame for making efforts, rather than to "reasonable" effort.

97. After discussion, the Commission agreed to retain the paragraph as drafted.

### 9. Article 9. Liability of holder

98. The Commission agreed to revise paragraph 2 as follows, on the understanding that the holder should also assume certain liability that was not ascertainable from the negotiable cargo document:

"A holder that is not the consignor and that exercises a right in accordance with article 7 assumes any liability:

(a) Attributable to the person exercising such a right under the law applicable to the transport contract; or

(b) That arises from the exercise of that right under the transport contract to the extent that such liability is ascertainable from the negotiable cargo document, as if it were a party to the transport contract".

### 10. Article 11. Transfer of rights incorporated in a negotiable cargo document

99. The Commission took up a suggestion to clarify the methods of transfer of the rights in a negotiable cargo document following the approach adopted in article 13 of the United Nations Convention on International Bills of Exchange and International Promissory Notes (1988).

100. It was observed that the words "incorporated in" should be replaced by "provided for" in line with the changes made in article 7 (see para. 89 above). It was suggested that the explanatory note should clarify that the same rights would be transferred from one holder to another.

101. A proposal to expand the provision to also address the liability being transferred to the holder did not receive support. It was mentioned that a holder might incur costs associated with the exercise of the aforementioned rights and that those costs should not be transferred from one holder to another.

102. After discussion, the Commission agreed to revise article 11 as follows:

"*Article 11. Transfer of the holder's rights*

The holder transfers the rights provided for in the negotiable cargo document to another person:

(a) By endorsement either to such person or in blank and by transferring possession of the negotiable cargo document to that person; or

(b) By mere transfer of possession of the negotiable cargo document to that person, if the last endorsement is in blank."

### 11. Article 12. Requirements for an electronic negotiable cargo document

103. The Commission did not take up a proposal to replace the word "issuance" with "signature" in paragraph 2. It was observed that the integrity of an electronic record should be assessed from a single point in time. It was added that, in the context of the convention, issuance was the more appropriate point, even though according to the definition of "negotiable cargo document" a signature was required. The general view was that the act of issuing a negotiable cargo document presupposed that it had been signed and put into circulation.

### 12. Article 13. Content requirements

104. It was suggested that article 13 of the draft convention be aligned with article 8 of the Model Law on Electronic Transferable Records by means of a reference to an "in writing" requirement. It was explained that the revision would clearly establish a functional equivalence rule, which was needed as the requirement for a signature in the definition of "negotiable cargo document" in article 2, paragraph 5, presupposed that a negotiable cargo document was in writing.

105. In response, it was noted that, while article 13 referred to a requirement for information to be contained in a negotiable cargo document, it was the same in substance as article 8 of the Model Law on Electronic Transferable Records. Attention was drawn to paragraph 47 of the Guide to Enactment of the UNCITRAL Model Law on Electronic Commerce (1996),[12] which equated a requirement for information to be "in writing" with a requirement for information to be contained in a paper-based "document". It was also pointed out that the convention adopted a "medium-neutral" approach insofar as it applied to electronic and paper-based negotiable cargo documents, as stated in the definition of "negotiable cargo document", and therefore did not necessarily require that such documents be "in writing". It was added that, unlike the Model Law on Electronic Transferable Records, which enabled the use of electronic transferable records by establishing a standard to meet the "in writing" requirements established under the law applicable to paper-based transferable documents, the convention itself established formal requirements that applied to electronic records, and it would be anachronistic to characterize any of those requirements as a requirement for the negotiable cargo document to be in writing.

106. It was observed that article 13 of the draft convention and article 8 of the Model Law on Electronic Transferable Records both addressed the same point, that the information contained in an electronic record needed to be "accessible so as to be usable for subsequent reference". Accordingly, an electronic records management system that supported the use of electronic transferable records by complying with the functional equivalence rule in the Model Law would likely meet the requirements under article 13, further supporting the use of e-negotiable cargo documents.

107. While there was some support for the proposal and for an alternative proposal to expressly refer to a negotiable cargo document being in writing, the prevailing view was that the current drafting was more appropriate. The Commission agreed to retain article 13 as drafted.

### 13. Article 15. Possession requirements

108. It was observed that the requirement to transfer possession was not only found in article 11 but also other provisions of the convention. The Commission therefore agreed to amend paragraph 2 as follows: "A requirement to transfer possession of a negotiable cargo document is met with respect to an electronic record through the transfer of control over the electronic record."

### 14. Article 17. Change of medium

109. A proposal was made to amend paragraph 2 to clarify that it did not impose an obligation on the transport operator to change medium but merely allowed it to make such a change. In response, it was noted that paragraph 1 applied when there was an agreement between the transport operator and the holder to change medium, in which case the transport operator should be obliged to change the medium as a consequence of that agreement. After discussion, the Commission did not take up the proposal.

110. A proposal was made to clarify the meaning of "change of medium". After discussion, it was agreed to amend paragraph 1 by inserting the words "from a paper document to an electronic record or from an electronic record to a paper document" after "negotiable cargo document".

111. A query was raised about the application of the law governing the underlying transport document, which might provide different rules for a change of medium. In response, it was suggested that the issue was already sufficiently addressed in the convention, particularly article 1, paragraph 3.

[12] General Assembly resolution 51/162, annex.

### 15. Article 18. General reliability standard

112. While suggestions were made to amend paragraph (a) to clarify the listed factors and how they would apply, the Commission agreed to retain the wording of article 18, which was based on article 12 of the Model Law on Electronic Transferable Records, as drafted.

### 16. No requirement to use an electronic negotiable cargo document

113. The Commission heard a proposal to include a provision stating that the convention did not require any person to use an electronic negotiable cargo document without that person's consent. It was explained that (a) a similar provision was found in existing UNCITRAL texts on electronic commerce, including article 7, paragraph 2, of the Model Law on Electronic Transferable Records; (b) such a provision would ensure party autonomy; and (c) some sectors or jurisdictions might not yet be ready to accept electronic methods and subsequent holders might have difficulty accessing the electronic records management system used to support a particular electronic negotiable cargo document.

114. While some support was expressed for the proposal, the necessity and desirability of the proposed provision was questioned as follows:

(a) Firstly, it was questioned whether the draft convention even required the parties to use a specific medium. It was observed that article 3, paragraph 1, already impliedly required the transport operator and the consignor to agree on the medium in which the negotiable cargo document was to be issued, and it was suggested that that requirement could be made explicit. It was also explained that article 17 was included precisely to allow a subsequent holder to accept an electronic negotiable cargo document with the security of knowing that it could switch to a paper-based version. The requirement for the transport operator to agree to the switch in all cases was reaffirmed;

(b) Secondly, it was observed that the convention was not concerned with the use of negotiable cargo document by other persons. Specifically, it was recalled that the acceptance of electronic negotiable cargo documents by customs and other public authorities was expressly beyond the scope of the convention by virtue of article 1, paragraph 2, and that the need of a consignee (as buyer) for the consignor (as seller) to procure the issuance of a paper negotiable cargo document was a matter for the relevant contract of sale of the goods, which was also beyond the scope of the convention by virtue of article 1, paragraph 1. It was said that that could be clarified in the explanatory note;

(c) Thirdly, a view was expressed that the proposed provision could create a hierarchy between paper and electronic negotiable cargo documents, which could undermine trade digitalization. It was added that, while a similar provision made sense in the Model Law on Electronic Transferable Records, it was not compatible with the medium-neutral approach taken in the convention.

In response, it was proposed that the provision could state in a medium-neutral manner that the convention did not require any person to use a negotiable cargo document in a paper or electronic form without that person's consent.

115. After discussion, the Commission agreed not to take up the proposal but to amend article 3, paragraph 1, by inserting the words "in the medium agreed upon" after "negotiable cargo document".

### 17. Final clauses

#### (a) Preserving existing regimes for transport involving a maritime leg

116. A proposal was made to insert a disconnection clause to exclude the application of the convention where the transport contract was governed by the United Nations Convention on Contracts for the International Carriage of Goods Wholly or Partly by

Sea[13] (the "Rotterdam Rules"). It was explained that the Rotterdam Rules contained overlapping provisions dealing with negotiable transport documents and reproduced the practice of maritime bills of lading. It was added that the Rotterdam Rules had been carefully drafted to ensure a balanced legal regime. In response, it was questioned why maritime transport should be treated differently from other modes of transport and it was noted that articles 7 and 9 of the draft convention had been revised to align more closely with the practice of maritime bills of lading. It was noted that the proposed provision was not so much a disconnection clause applicable among States Parties to the Rotterdam Rules but rather an exclusion from scope. A concern was also raised about yielding to the Rotterdam Rules, which were not yet in force. In view of there being a strong interest in promoting the Rotterdam Rules, a suggestion was made to clarify in the explanatory note that becoming a State Party to the convention on negotiable cargo documents in no way prevented a State from subsequently signing or ratifying the Rotterdam Rules.

117. The Commission heard proposals to insert a provision allowing reservations. A view was expressed that, even in the absence of a specific provision on reservations, States would retain the ability to formulate them, as recognized under article 19 of the Vienna Convention on the Law of Treaties. In that regard, it was pointed out that formulating a reservation that was incompatible with the object and purpose of a convention would not be allowed, and views were expressed that formulating a reservation to exclude negotiable transport documents that covered maritime transport in either a unimodal or multimodal context might defeat the purpose of establishing a uniform law regime covering all modes of transport.

118. One proposal was to insert a general provision allowing States to make any type of reservation, subject to acceptance by State Parties under a silence procedure. It was said that, alternatively, the convention need not include any provision on reservations. It was noted that both a provision along the lines proposed and the absence of such a provision would offer States flexibility in applying the convention while maintaining existing national law and treaty regimes applicable to bills of lading.

119. Another proposal was made to introduce a provision allowing a State to declare that it would not apply the convention to any negotiable transport document that evidenced or contained a contract which, under the law of that State, was governed by an international convention that applied to contracts for the carriage of goods by sea or by inland waterway, in which case the convention would not apply to a negotiable transport document that evidenced or contained a contract governed by the law of the declaring State.

120. It was observed that the above-mentioned provision would cover a wide range of negotiable transport documents, including those used for multimodal transport. It was suggested that such a broad exclusion should not be permitted, as it would undermine the key objective of facilitating the multimodal transport of goods. Several concerns were raised about the effects of the proposed provision. Firstly, it was observed that whether or not a particular contract was governed by an international convention should not be determined under the law of the declaring State but, rather, pursuant to the provisions of the relevant convention. Secondly, it was observed that the determination as to whether or not the exclusion applied would depend on a complex conflict of laws analysis, which would be complicated by uncertainty as to whether that analysis should apply to the negotiable transport document or to the underlying transport contract. Thirdly, it was observed that that would result in a State other than a declaring State not applying the convention if the conflict of laws analysis led to the conclusion that the law of the declaring State applied, and it was questioned whether that was a desirable outcome, particularly for other States wanting to apply the convention in full.

[13] General Assembly resolution 63/122, annex.

121. After discussion, the Commission was invited to consider including a new article reading as follows:

> "1. Any State may declare, at the time of the deposit of its instrument of ratification, acceptance, approval or accession or at any time thereafter, that it will not apply this Convention to any negotiable transport document that evidences or contains a contract for the carriage of goods by sea governed by an international convention to which it is a State Party.
>
> 2. No reservations are permitted except that expressly authorized in this article."

122. It was observed that, by purporting to exclude certain types of negotiable transport documents from the application of the convention, a declaration made by a State under the article would constitute a reservation within the meaning of article 2 (d) of the Vienna Convention on the Law of Treaties. It was also observed that the proposed article referred to a declaration being made "at any time" after ratification, acceptance, approval or accession, while the Vienna Convention on the Law of Treaties only referred to reservations being formulated at the time of signature, ratification, acceptance, approval or accession. In response, it was noted that negotiating States were free to allow reservations to be formulated at a later time.

123. Preference was expressed for the inclusion of the new article on reservations in lieu of the disconnection clause and proposed reservation clauses (see paras. 116–119 above). It was further stressed that the reservation would be permitted only with regard to unimodal maritime contracts governed by international conventions. It was explained that the phrase "carriage of goods by sea" was intended to refer to "wholly" by sea and could be further clarified. A view was expressed that paragraph 2 should not be included to provide full flexibility to States in formulating reservations. In response, it was observed that States should be allowed to formulate reservations only under well-defined circumstances and that paragraph 2 should be retained.

124. After discussion, the Commission agreed to include a new article on reservations referred to in paragraph 121 above and to replace the words "by sea" with "wholly by sea" to clarify that the reservation was limited to unimodal maritime transport. However, views were expressed that the inclusion of paragraph 2 of the new article had not been the subject of sufficient substantive debate. The Commission also agreed to include a provision addressing the procedure for and effects of reservations, as well as withdrawals.

### (b) Entry into force

125. The Commission agreed that the number of instruments of ratification, acceptance, approval or accession required to bring the convention into force should be 10, and therefore agreed to replace the word "third" in article 24 with "tenth".

### (c) Other matters

126. The Commission welcomed a statement by the Government of Ghana expressing its interest in hosting a signing ceremony for the convention, possibly in 2026, after its adoption by the General Assembly.

127. The Commission also welcomed a statement by the European Bank for Reconstruction and Development commending the Commission for its work on the convention and affirming its support in promoting the convention, including through its Trade Facilitation Programme.

## C. Approval of the draft convention

128. At its 1243rd meeting, on 11 July 2025, the Commission adopted by consensus the following decision and recommendation to the General Assembly:

"*The United Nations Commission on International Trade Law,*

"*Recalling* its mandate under General Assembly resolution 2205 (XXI) of 17 December 1966 to further the progressive harmonization and unification of the law of international trade and in that respect to bear in mind the interests of all peoples, in particular those of developing countries, in the extensive development of international trade,

"*Conscious* of the important role played by negotiable transport documents in facilitating trade finance and the sale of goods in transit,

"*Convinced* of the desirability of establishing uniform rules for negotiable transport documents covering all modes of transport, including multimodal transport, thereby supporting the growth of door-to-door transportation,

"*Acknowledging* that digital transformation in international trade depends on reliable systems and data, which in turn can enhance operational efficiency and support end-to-end digitalization,

"*Convinced* that certainty with regard to the legal effect of negotiable cargo documents, as well as the rights and liability of the holder, will encourage the acceptance of such documents by banks, financial institutions and other stakeholders, thereby fostering international trade and contributing to economic growth,

"*Convinced also* that a sound legal framework could help reduce the costs of trade along inland routes and will assist both landlocked countries and countries with large mainland territories in integrating more effectively into global supply chains,

"*Noting* that the preparation of the draft convention on negotiable cargo documents was the subject of due deliberation in the Commission and that the draft convention benefited from consultations with Governments and interested intergovernmental and international non-governmental organizations,

"*Noting also* that the text of the draft convention was circulated for comment before the fifty-eighth session of the Commission to all Governments invited to attend the meetings of the Commission and its Working Group VI (Negotiable Cargo Documents) as members and observers,

"*Expressing* its appreciation to the International Civil Aviation Organization, the Intergovernmental Organization for International Carriage by Rail and the Organization for Cooperation between Railways for their assistance in the preparation of the draft convention,

"*Having considered* the draft convention and the comments submitted by Governments and international organizations at its fifty-eighth session, in 2025,

"1. *Submits* to the General Assembly the draft convention on negotiable cargo documents, as it appears in annex I to the report of the United Nations Commission on International Trade Law on the work of its fifty-eighth session;[14]

"2. *Recommends* that the General Assembly, taking into account the extensive consideration given to the draft convention by the Commission and its Working Group VI (Negotiable Cargo Documents), consider the draft convention with a view to adopting, at its eightieth session, on the basis of the

---

[14] *Official Records of the General Assembly, Eightieth Session, Supplement No. 17* (A/80/17), annex I.

draft convention approved by the Commission, the United Nations Convention on Negotiable Cargo Documents;

"3. *Requests* the Secretary-General to publish the Convention, upon adoption, including electronically and in the six official languages of the United Nations, and to disseminate it broadly to Governments and other interested bodies."

# V. Finalization and adoption of the UNCITRAL Toolkit and Background Notes on Asset Tracing and Recovery in Insolvency Proceedings

## A. General

129. The Commission recalled that, at its fifty-fourth session, in 2021, it had mandated its Working Group V to undertake work on the topic of asset tracing and recovery in insolvency proceedings,[15] and that the Working Group had commenced work on that topic at its fifty-ninth session. The Commission was informed that the Working Group, at its sixty-fifth session, had agreed for the UNCITRAL secretariat to circulate the draft toolkit for expedited asset tracing and recovery in insolvency proceedings and the draft background notes on asset tracing and recovery in insolvency proceedings, as revised to reflect its deliberations and decisions at that session, for comment by States (A/CN.9/1198, para. 25). It was further informed that the Working Group, at its sixty-sixth session, had concluded its work on the topic and had agreed to recommend the draft toolkit and background notes as contained in document A/CN.9/WG.V/WP.201 with the amendments set out in the report of that session (A/CN.9/1203, chap. IV) for consideration, finalization and adoption by the Commission at its fifty-eighth session (A/CN.9/1203, para. 24).

130. Pursuant to that recommendation, the Commission, at its current session, considered the draft toolkit and background notes, as contained in document A/CN.9/WG.V/WP.201 and amended by the Working Group at its sixty-sixth session (A/CN.9/1203, chap. IV) (the "draft texts"). It also had before it the comments received from States on the draft toolkit and background notes contained in document A/CN.9/WG.V/WP.201 (A/CN.9/1221 and A/CN.9/1221/Add.1).

131. The Commission took note of general comments by States related to the agenda item, including expressions of appreciation to: (a) the delegation that had proposed the topic to the Commission; (b) the Working Group and the secretariat for preparing the draft texts and ensuring their high quality, clarity, relevance to various stakeholders and comprehensive and inclusive scope, reflecting different legal systems; and (c) the Chair of the Working Group for his able stewardship of the Working Group's deliberations on the topic. The Commission agreed to include a table of contents for the entire publication. It welcomed the announcement of the upcoming enactment of the UNCITRAL Model Law on Cross-Border Insolvency (1997)[16] by a State and also welcomed the finalization and adoption of the draft texts at the current session as timely and relevant in that context.

## B. Decision on the adoption of the UNCITRAL Toolkit and Background Notes on Asset Tracing and Recovery in Insolvency Proceedings

132. As no comments were made at the session regarding the substance of the draft texts, the Commission adopted the texts with no substantive changes, under the title "Asset Tracing and Recovery in Insolvency Proceedings: UNCITRAL Toolkit and Background Notes", with a table of contents for the entire publication added. It agreed

[15] Ibid., *Seventy-sixth Session, Supplement No. 17* (A/76/17), paras. 215–217.

[16] General Assembly resolution 52/158, annex.

that the adopted texts would be published in the six official languages of the United Nations, including electronically.

133. The Commission emphasized the relevance of the adopted texts for the protection, preservation and maximization of the value of the insolvency estate for the benefit of all creditors and other parties in interest, including the debtor and its employees. It noted that, by complementing and supplementing the UNCITRAL insolvency framework, the adopted texts would support an environment conducive to trade and business, promote access to credit and encourage investment. The texts would also contribute to broader socioeconomic objectives, including the promotion of the rule of law and good governance.

134. It was observed that the adopted texts could be of practical value to judges, insolvency practitioners and other stakeholders in situations involving asset tracing and recovery. In particular, the texts might facilitate court-to-court communication and cooperation and expedite asset tracing and recovery across borders, whether or not in the context of insolvency, and in both physical and digital settings. The Commission appreciated that the complexities arising from asset tracing and recovery in the digital environment, namely owing to the ease of movement of digital assets and the instantaneous conclusion of multiple and numerous transactions whose parties might not be (immediately or easily) identifiable, had been duly taken into account in the preparation of the texts by the Working Group. It also appreciated that the relevant Hague conventions had been taken into account in preparing the texts.

135. The Commission also expressed confidence that policymakers and legislators would find the adopted texts useful for assessing the availability, accessibility, effectiveness and efficiency of their domestic legal and institutional frameworks for asset tracing and recovery. The results of such assessments could inform the need to enhance domestic frameworks with new asset tracing and recovery tools or to introduce other changes in response to evolving challenges and opportunities, especially those arising in the digital environment.

136. Accordingly, the Commission requested the secretariat to ensure the wide dissemination of the adopted texts in the six official languages of the United Nations, so as to enhance their visibility and accessibility and facilitate their use by all relevant stakeholders. It expressed appreciation to all States, organizations and individual experts whose contributions had proved crucial for the quality of the adopted texts.

# VI. Finalization and adoption of the UNCITRAL Toolkit on Prevention and Mitigation of International Investment Disputes

## A. Introduction

137. The Commission recalled that at its fifty-seventh session, it had noted the progress made with regard to a toolkit on prevention and mitigation of international investment disputes.[17] At that session, the secretariat had been requested to circulate the draft toolkit (A/CN.9/1185) for comments and feedback by States, on the basis of which an updated version of the toolkit could be prepared and presented to the Commission for finalization.[18]

138. It was further recalled that the work on the toolkit had been undertaken by Working Group III during its thirty-ninth,[19] forty-fifth,[20] forty-seventh[21] and

[17] Ibid., *Seventy-eighth Session, Supplement No. 17* (A/78/17), paras. 168 and 169.

[18] Ibid.

[19] See A/CN.9/1044, paras. 17–26.

[20] See A/CN.9/1131, paras. 46–52.

[21] See A/CN.9/1161, para. 112. At that session, Working Group considered the draft guidelines on

forty-eighth sessions and that the toolkit had also been the subject of intensive intersessional consultations.[22]

139. At the current session, the Commission had before it the draft toolkit on prevention and mitigation of international investment disputes (A/CN.9/1220), which had been prepared taking into account the comments and feedback received from States.[23]

## B. Consideration of the draft toolkit

140. At the outset, the Commission acknowledged the importance of dispute prevention and mitigation, and the value of the toolkit as a practical resource for States and other stakeholders involved in investor-State dispute settlement. The Commission also expressed appreciation to the secretariat for compiling and incorporating the feedback received from States.

141. It was noted that the draft toolkit had been prepared as a non-prescriptive document that could be updated to reflect the evolving practices and experiences of States in preventing and managing investment disputes, and that the relevance of the toolkit was enhanced by the inclusion of concrete examples, practices and lessons learned from recent dispute prevention efforts.

142. The Commission agreed that the draft toolkit should be amended as follows:

(a) A footnote should be added in the first sentence of paragraph 3, to read: "This does not mean that regional economic integration organizations are States. However, regional economic integration organizations may, depending on their structure and the scope of their regulatory authority, engage the strategies or impose the measures listed in the Toolkit.";

(b) The first part of the third sentence of paragraph 12 should read: "However, facilitating access to, and providing such information, may not create any expectation on the part of investors, as investors should conduct due diligence…";

(c) The last sentence of paragraph 19 should read: "In Argentina at the national level, draft laws are published on the congressional website, and there are some mechanisms that allow for public participation as well as specific examples of ex ante evaluation of regulatory projects.";

(d) Given that the term "grievance mechanism" was used broadly to cover feedback mechanisms, and as reference was being made to the practice of the World Bank, the third sentence of paragraph 23 should read: "A grievance mechanism provides investors who consider themselves to have been negatively affected with a process to voice their concerns.";

(e) The second sentence of paragraph 66 should be deleted.

143. In addition, a number of clarifications and corrections were provided regarding State practices (referred to in the body of the toolkit, the footnotes and section F). States were invited to submit any further corrections or updates to the secretariat by 29 August 2025 so that the secretariat could reflect the corrections in the final version of the toolkit.

144. The Commission further agreed that it would be useful for the toolkit to be updated periodically to reflect new and emerging practices. It was agreed that the secretariat would report back to the Commission when it was appropriate to prepare

prevention and mitigation of international investment disputes based on document A/CN.9/WG.III/WP.235.

[22] At its forty-eighth session, Working Group considered an informal revised version of the draft guidelines.

[23] Comments received from States are available at https://uncitral.un.org/en/investmentmediationanddisputeprevention in the language in which they were received.

a revised version of the Toolkit based on the information gathered. For that purpose, States were requested to provide relevant information to the secretariat as appropriate.

### C. Decision on the adoption of the UNCITRAL Toolkit on Prevention and Mitigation of International Investment Disputes

145. At its 1254th meeting, on 21 July 2025, the Commission adopted by consensus the UNCITRAL Toolkit on Prevention and Mitigation of International Investment Disputes, consisting of the text contained in document A/CN.9/1220 with amendments based on the deliberations and decisions of the Commission (see paras. 142 and 143 above). The Commission authorized the secretariat to finalize the text of the Toolkit pursuant to the decisions of the Commission.

146. The Commission agreed to recommend the use of the UNCITRAL Toolkit on Prevention and Mitigation of International Investment Disputes by States, investors, public officials, dispute prevention units, legal advisers, institutions and other relevant stakeholders in supporting the development and implementation of effective strategies to prevent and mitigate international investment disputes.

147. The Commission further requested the Secretary-General to publish the UNCITRAL Toolkit on Prevention and Mitigation of International Investment Disputes, including electronically, in the six official languages of the United Nations, and disseminate it broadly to Governments and other interested bodies.

## VII. Approval for publication of the model organization rules for limited liability enterprises

148. The Commission had before it the draft model organization rules for limited liability enterprises (A/CN.9/1228), which had been prepared by the secretariat pursuant to the Commission's deliberations at its fifty-fourth session. It was recalled that at that session, the Commission had adopted the UNCITRAL Legislative Guide on Limited Liability Enterprises, providing a simplified legal form for micro-, small and medium-sized enterprises. It had also instructed the secretariat to prepare guidance, with the assistance of experts, to support States in developing model rules to assist limited liability enterprise members – particularly those with limited legal resources – in drafting organization rules for the internal management of their limited liability enterprises in a fair, effective and transparent manner. It was further recalled that given the emphasis in the Legislative Guide on contractual freedom in the governance of micro-, small and medium-sized enterprises, organization rules were a core feature of the limited liability enterprise form, allowing entrepreneurs to tailor governance arrangements to their specific needs subject to the domestic provisions implementing the mandatory rules of the Legislative Guide and other applicable laws.

149. The Commission noted that the guidance prepared by the secretariat in the form of the model organization rules comprised two templates, each differing in scope and structure to accommodate the varying needs of entrepreneurs. While both templates were suitable for single-member and multi-member limited liability enterprises, one was intended for limited liability enterprises managed by all members or designated managers, and offered a comprehensive format with selectable options (a "check-the-box" approach) for users seeking greater guidance. The other, designed for member-managed limited liability enterprises, was more concise, with minimal predefined choices, and was intended for users more familiar with enterprise governance. The Commission noted the secretariat's suggestion that, in view of the differences in format and intended use, both templates be endorsed.

150. The Commission recalled that the draft templates were derived from the Legislative Guide and noted that the templates were intended to serve as guidance for

States, which could further adapt them to align them more closely with their domestic legal frameworks. The Commission agreed as follows:

(a) Paragraph 2 (h) of the draft model organization rules would be modified to read: "events leading to the dissolution of the LLE", as that wording more accurately reflected the guidance provided in paragraph 134 of the Legislative Guide;

(b) Provision 1.2 in both template one and template two should include a footnote clarifying in what circumstances reference to the "precise geographical location" of the limited liability enterprise might be needed;

(c) Provision 6.3.1 in template one would be deleted, as the subject matter was addressed in provision 13;

(d) The phrase "otherwise recorded notice" in provision 7.3 in both template one and template two would be replaced with "notice otherwise communicated";

(e) The first two options in provision 8.4 in template one ("☐ A rotation voting (deciding vote rotates among the members); ☐ A dispute resolution") would be deleted;

(f) The phrase "there shall be either a rotation voting (deciding vote rotates among members) or a dispute resolution" in provision 8.4 in template two would be replaced with a placeholder reading "[specify which method]".

151. Following its consideration of the text, the Commission endorsed both templates prepared by the secretariat, subject to the changes referred to in paragraph 150 (a) to (f) above, and authorized the secretariat to make any further editorial adjustments thereto, as necessary to enhance clarity. In addition to using the templates as a basis for preparing model rules, the Commission noted that States could also make them directly accessible to members of limited liability enterprises, where appropriate. The Commission further authorized the secretariat to make the templates available, in the six official languages of the United Nations, electronically on the UNCITRAL website and to publish them as an annex to the *UNCITRAL Legislative Guide on Limited Liability Enterprises*.

# VIII. Approval for publication of the UNCITRAL-UNIDROIT study on the legal nature of verified carbon credits issued by independent carbon standard setters

152. The Commission recalled that at its fifty-fourth session, it had heard a proposal to examine: (a) how existing UNCITRAL texts could be aligned with climate change mitigation, adaptation and resilience goals; and (b) whether further work could be done by UNCITRAL to facilitate those goals in the implementation of those texts or through the development of new texts. The Commission also heard at that session that legal uncertainty regarding the legal status of carbon credits traded in voluntary carbon markets could be a focus for future legislative work.[24]

153. The Commission further recalled that, at its fifty-seventh session, it had considered the UNCITRAL-UNIDROIT study on the legal nature of verified carbon credits issued by independent carbon standard setters as contained in document A/CN.9/1191.[25] The Commission had requested the secretariat to circulate

[24] *Official Records of the General Assembly, Seventy-sixth Session, Supplement No. 17* (A/76/17), para. 244. Summaries of the Commission's deliberations during its fifty-fifth and fifty-sixth sessions can be found respectively in ibid., *Seventy-seventh Session, Supplement No. 17* (A/77/17), paras. 209–216, and in ibid., *Seventy-eighth Session, Supplement No. 17* (A/78/17), paras. 186–199.

[25] Ibid., *Seventy-ninth Session, Supplement No. 17* (A/79/17), paras. 272–274. To reflect the comments received on document A/CN.9/1191, a revised version of the study (A/CN.9/1191/Rev.1) was prepared by the secretariat following the fifty-seventh session and circulated to all States Members of the United Nations on 17 September 2024 for additional comments.

the study to all States Members of the United Nations and give them sufficient time to provide comments, with a view to compiling those comments and submitting them, together with the study, for consideration at the current session. The Commission had agreed to hold a further discussion on the findings of the study, as well as the issues highlighted by States in their comments, and to consider whether to request the secretariat to prepare a revised version of the study for publication.[26]

154. The Commission had before it the study (A/CN.9/1191/Rev.1) and a compilation of comments on the study (A/CN.9/1216 and A/CN.9/1216/Add.1–3). The Commission expressed its appreciation to the secretariats of UNCITRAL and UNIDROIT for the preparation of the study, acknowledging the amount of effort put into it and noting that it had benefited from input from various States and stakeholders. The Commission also welcomed the comments by States and international organizations, which were elaborated upon during the discussions. The value and usefulness of the study was recognized, as it identified various legal issues with regard to verified carbon credits and could assist States and other stakeholders in considering and dealing with those issues.

155. During the deliberations, questions were raised with respect to: (a) the scope of the study, including the need to cover carbon credit schemes administered by public authorities, as well as approaches and mechanisms under article 6 of the Paris Agreement; (b) the characterization of the mechanism under article 6.4 of the Paris Agreement in the study; (c) whether verified "carbon" credits was the appropriate terminology to use, as it focused on emissions of carbon dioxide and not other greenhouse gases; (d) whether UNCITRAL was the appropriate forum for the work; (e) whether there might be a risk of fragmentation or overlap with work being done under the United Nations Framework Convention on Climate Change; and (f) whether and how the study should be updated to reflect the comments received. With respect to the last point, it was suggested that the secretariat update the study by incorporating the technical comments therein while reproducing more general or policy-related comments in an annex thereto. It was clarified that the secretariat would communicate with States or organizations that had submitted comments on whether they wished to have their comments included in the annex. States and organizations were invited to submit any additional comments on the study by 29 August 2025 so that they could be reflected in the revised version.

156. After discussion, the Commission requested the secretariat to prepare a revised version of the study, which would reflect the relevant deliberations of the Commission at its current session, incorporate the technical comments received and include in an annex the policy-related comments received, and to make the revised version of the study available on the website of the Commission in the six official languages of the United Nations, resources permitting. The Commission noted that the publication of the study on its website would conclude its work on the legal nature of verified carbon credits.

# IX. Approval for publication of the guidance document on legal issues relating to the use of distributed ledger technology in trade

157. The Commission had before it the draft guidance document on legal issues relating to the use of distributed ledger technology in trade (A/CN.9/1222), which had been prepared pursuant to a request by the Commission at its fifty-fifth session (A/77/17, paras. 22 (f) and 169).

158. It was explained that the document provided guidance on legal issues arising in relation to the procurement of distributed ledger technology services for commercial purposes and the use of distributed ledger technology in the delivery of commercial services, and illustrated the use of distributed ledger technology in connection with UNCITRAL texts.

[26] Ibid., para. 274.

159. It was recalled that at its fifty-sixth session, the Commission had considered a paper on the scope of that work and had noted its intersection with other digital trade workstreams of UNCITRAL (A/78/17, paras. 200–202). It was also recalled that at its fifty-seventh session, the Commission had considered a note that established a link between the use of distributed ledger technology and UNCITRAL texts (A/79/17, paras. 286–290).

160. Broad appreciation was expressed for the guidance document, and it was suggested that it could be published online in the same format as the *Notes on the Main Issues of Cloud Computing Contracts.*[27] It was noted that the descriptive elements of decentralized autonomous organizations set out in document A/CN.9/1225 could complement the guidance document. It was also suggested that the concept of "trustless" distributed ledgers could be clarified in light of the various references to trust-building mechanisms contained in the guidance document.

161. After discussion, the Commission welcomed the draft guidance document on legal issues relating to the use of distributed ledger technology in trade as contained in document A/CN.9/1222 and authorized its publication, with the incorporation of the descriptive elements of decentralized autonomous organizations set out in A/CN.9/1225, in electronic form in the six official languages of the United Nations.

## X. Dispute settlement: progress report of Working Group II

162. The Commission recalled that, at its fifty-seventh session, it had adopted the UNCITRAL Model Clauses on Specialized Express Dispute Resolution[28] and had approved in principle the draft explanatory notes thereto, as contained in document A/CN.9/1181. It had further requested Working Group II to edit and finalize the draft explanatory notes on the basis of the Commission's decisions and deliberations.[29] Accordingly, the Working Group had finalized the Explanatory Notes at its eightieth session (A/CN.9/1193, paras. 13–42).

163. The Commission also recalled that, at the same session, it had mandated the Working Group to work on the recognition and enforcement of electronic arbitral awards and, subsequently, on electronic notices. In that regard, the Commission had provided the Working Group with a broad mandate to identify the issues and explore appropriate solutions, without prejudice to the final form of the outcome. The Commission had also requested the secretariat to organize a two-day colloquium during the eightieth session of the Working Group with the aim of obtaining perspectives in order to assess the issues with respect to electronic awards and contemplate possible solutions for electronic notices of arbitration. The Commission had further requested the secretariat to conduct preparatory work for the topic of the recognition and enforcement of electronic arbitral awards for consideration by the Working Group.[30] Accordingly, at its eightieth session, the Working Group had held a two-day colloquium and had commenced deliberations on the topic of the recognition and enforcement of electronic arbitral awards on the basis of the notes prepared by the secretariat (A/CN.9/1190 and A/CN.9/WG.II/WP.238). The Working Group had continued those deliberations at its eighty-first session on the basis of a note prepared by the secretariat (A/CN.9/WG.II/WP.240).

164. At the current session, the Commission had before it the reports of Working Group II on the work of its eightieth session (Vienna, 30 September–4 October 2024)

---

[27] United Nations, *Notes on the Main Issues of Cloud Computing Contracts* (prepared by the secretariat of the United Nations Commission on International Trade Law, 2019), New York, 2019.

[28] *Official Records of the General Assembly, Seventy-ninth Session*, Supplement No. 17 (A/79/17), annex II.

[29] Ibid., *Seventy-ninth Session, Supplement No. 17* (A/79/17), paras. 93 and 265 (b).

[30] Ibid., paras. 284 and 285.

(A/CN.9/1193) and its eighty-first session (New York, 3–7 February 2025) (A/CN.9/1200).

165. A view was expressed that the Working Group should ensure that arbitral awards in electronic form met sufficiently rigorous requirements with respect to performance of the same functions as paper-based awards. In response, it was said that such requirements should not be more stringent than those applicable to paper-based awards, and that the Working Group had made good progress in striking an appropriate balance between functionality and safeguards, which would continue to guide the work going forward.

166. After discussion, the Commission expressed its satisfaction with the progress made on the topic of the recognition and enforcement of electronic arbitral awards and commended the Working Group for finalizing the Explanatory Notes to the UNCITRAL Model Clauses on Specialized Express Dispute Resolution. The Commission also expressed its appreciation for the support provided by the secretariat.

# XI. Investor-State dispute settlement reform: progress report of Working Group III

167. The Commission recalled that, at its fiftieth session, in 2017, it had entrusted Working Group III with a broad mandate to work on the possible reform of investor-State dispute settlement.[31] The Commission also recalled that: (a) at its fifty-sixth session, it had finalized and adopted the first set of investor-State dispute settlement reform elements recommended by the Working Group, which included the codes of conduct and texts on mediation;[32] and (b) at its fifty-seventh session, it had adopted in principle the Statute of the Advisory Centre on International Investment Dispute Resolution.[33]

168. Taking note of the reports of Working Group III on the work of the forty-ninth, fiftieth, and first and second parts of the fifty-first sessions (A/CN.9/1194, A/CN.9/1195, A/CN.9/1196 and A/CN.9/1196/Add.1), the Commission commended the Working Group for making progress on a number of investor-State dispute settlement reform elements, which included the draft provisions on procedural and cross-cutting issues, a draft statute of a standing mechanism for the resolution of international investment disputes (including an appellate mechanism) and a draft multilateral instrument on investor-State dispute settlement reform.

169. The Commission noted that progress had been facilitated through a series of intersessional and other informal meetings.[34] Reference was made to the eighth intersessional meeting, held in Chengdu, China, in October 2024, at which the topics of an appellate mechanism and a multilateral instrument on investor-State dispute settlement reform had been addressed.[35] It was noted that the ninth intersessional meeting, on procedural and cross-cutting issues, was scheduled to be held in Santiago from 5 to 7 November 2025 (A/CN.9/1195, para. 133).

170. The Commission recalled that the General Assembly had decided, on 24 December 2021, to allocate an additional one-week session per year to the Commission and the necessary human resources to the secretariat to support the work

[31] Ibid., *Seventy-second Session, Supplement No. 17* (A/72/17), para. 264.

[32] Ibid., *Seventy-eighth Session, Supplement No. 17* (A/78/17), chap. IV.

[33] Ibid., *Seventy-ninth Session, Supplement No. 17* (A/79/17), para. 167.

[34] Information about informal meetings is available on the web page of Working Group III (https://uncitral.un.org/en/working_groups/3/investor-state) in the right-hand column under "Inter-sessional Activities".

[35] See A/CN.9/WG.III/WP.249, "Summary of the intersessional meeting on investor-State dispute settlement reform submitted by the Government of China" (eighth intersessional meeting held on 24 and 25 October 2024 in Chengdu, China). Additional information about the meeting is available at https://uncitral.un.org/en/8thintersessional.

of Working Group III.[36] The Commission further recalled that, when it had made the recommendation to the General Assembly for the additional resources, it had decided to re-evaluate and, if needed, revisit its decision concerning the need to allocate an additional one-week session per year and supporting resources to the Working Group, taking into consideration the Working Group's report on the use of its resources.[37]

171. Accordingly, the Commission was informed that the additional conference time of one week allocated for 2025 had been utilized by Working Group III to hold the one-week fiftieth session in Vienna in January 2025.[38] In addition, the Commission recalled that it had decided to assign extra days for the Working Group to hold the first part of its fifty-first session in New York in February 2025.[39] It was observed that the additional conference time had allowed the Working Group to complete the first reading of the draft provisions on procedural and cross-cutting issues, a standing mechanism (including an appellate mechanism) and a multilateral instrument on investor-State dispute settlement reform. The Commission was further informed that two of the three additional posts allocated in 2022 had been filled, while one of the posts had been vacant since October 2023 due to the secondment of the staff member and the subsequent hiring restrictions. Lastly, the Commission was informed that the additional resources allocated by the General Assembly to support the work of Working Group III would expire at the end of 2025 (for further information on the possible extension of the resources, see chap. XVI, sect. E).

172. Referring to the updated workplan of Working Group III contained in document A/CN.9/1217, the Chair of the Working Group provided an outline of the work to be conducted by the Working Group during the sessions scheduled to be held before the fifty-ninth session of the Commission. It was indicated that the Working Group would aim to present reforms relating to procedural and cross-cutting issues and a standing mechanism for consideration by the Commission at its next session.

173. The Commission noted the secretariat's participation in events organized by UNCTAD, the International Centre for Settlement of Investment Disputes and the Organisation for Economic Co-operation and Development (OECD), and its efforts to hold a number of side events during the sessions of the Working Group, involving a large number of international governmental and non-governmental organizations.

174. The Commission was informed that the outcome document of the Fourth International Conference on Financing for Development (Sevilla, Spain, 30 June–3 July 2025), entitled "Sevilla Commitment", which had been submitted to the General Assembly for endorsement through a draft resolution, referred indirectly to the work of Working Group III by stating that the Conference resolved to support efforts to reform the mechanisms for investor-State dispute settlement in trade and investment agreements, including through a multilateral approach towards the establishment of the Advisory Centre on International Investment Dispute Resolution, and building on the ongoing work of the Commission.

175. The Commission further noted the outreach activities carried out by the secretariat to raise awareness about investor-State dispute settlement reform and to ensure that the reform process remained inclusive and fully transparent. The Commission also commended the secretariat for updating the Working Group III web page to provide relevant information in a concise and timely manner.

176. The Commission expressed its appreciation for the financial support provided by the Governments of France and Germany, the European Union and the Swiss Agency for Development and Cooperation. Noting and expressing its appreciation for the proposed financial contribution by the Government of Switzerland to support investor-State dispute settlement reforms, the Commission called for continued

---

[36] General Assembly resolution 76/229, para. 15.

[37] *Official Records of the General Assembly, Seventy-sixth Session, Supplement No. 17* (A/76/17), para. 263.

[38] Ibid., *Seventy-ninth Session, Supplement No. 17* (A/79/17), para. 375.

[39] Ibid., para. 163.

financial support by donors for travel and simultaneous interpretation to ensure the inclusiveness of the Working Group deliberations, and for post-related costs to enhance the capacity of the secretariat, including with regard to the implementation of investor-State dispute settlement reforms.

177. After discussion, the Commission expressed its satisfaction with the progress made by Working Group III and commended the secretariat for the support it provided to the Working Group.

# XII. Electronic commerce: progress report of Working Group IV

178. The Commission had before it the reports of Working Group IV on the work of its sixty-seventh session (Vienna, 18–22 November 2024) (A/CN.9/1197) and its sixty-eighth session (New York, 24–28 March 2025) (A/CN.9/1202). It noted with appreciation the progress made by the Working Group at those sessions, including its review of the draft guide to enactment of the UNCITRAL Model Law on Automated Contracting[40] (2024), as requested by the Commission at its fifty-seventh session,[41] and its advancing work on a draft set of default rules for data provision contracts.

179. The Commission observed that, following its review of the draft guide to enactment, the Working Group had discharged its mandate on the topic of the use of artificial intelligence and automation in contracting, as given by the Commission at its fifty-fifth session.[42] It also noted that the topic of data provision contracts was the sole substantive item on the agenda of the Working Group, and that the Working Group had heard an exchange of views, at its sixty-seventh session, on possible recommendations to the Commission on future work on legal issues related to digital trade. The Commission heard that digital platforms and other new means of trading, which had been presented to the Working Group, were the subject of proposals before the Commission at the current session (see chap. XVI, sect. C.3). Attention was also drawn to intersections between work on data provision contracts and other international initiatives on data governance and cross-border data flows, including as a result of the Global Digital Compact adopted by the General Assembly in 2024. The Commission heard that the secretariat was continuing to monitor those initiatives. The importance of ongoing work for promoting efforts related to data governance and cross-border data flows was stressed.

# XIII. Insolvency law: progress report of Working Group V

180. The Commission had before it the reports of Working Group V on the work of its sixty-fifth session (Vienna, 16–20 December 2024) (A/CN.9/1198) and its sixty-sixth session (New York, 12–16 May 2025) (A/CN.9/1203). It noted with appreciation the progress made by the Working Group at those sessions, including the finalization of its work on the topic of asset tracing and recovery in insolvency proceedings (see chap. V of the present report), as well as the fact that the Working Group's consideration of the topic of applicable law in insolvency proceedings had reached an advanced stage.

181. With respect to the latter topic, the Commission was informed that the Working Group had yet to make policy choices on several issues, including the law governing the effects of insolvency proceedings on the treatment of rights in rem or secured creditors in insolvency proceedings and the treatment of avoidance and set-off rights, close-out netting arrangements, arbitration agreements, and the intersection between insolvency and other proceedings, in particular litigation and arbitration (pending, ongoing and post-commencement).

---

[40] Ibid., annex IV.

[41] Ibid., para. 239.

[42] Ibid, *Seventy-seventh Session, Supplement No. 17* (A/77/17), para. 159.

182. The Commission was informed that the law governing the effects of insolvency proceedings on the treatment of rights in rem or secured creditors in insolvency proceedings was one of the most complex. It noted that unresolved issues included whether or not a proposed safeguard, namely the application of the insolvency law of the State where the asset was situated (*lex rei sitae*) as an exception to the default application of the law of the State in which the insolvency proceedings were commenced (*lex fori concursus*), should be limited to immovable property, and whether and how to address adequate protection of creditors within that safeguard. Related issues included the appropriate localization rules and the definition of "*lex rei sitae*", or alternatively, the use of the phrase "law governing the secured claim/right in rem".

183. The Commission was further informed that novel issues had arisen in the most recent deliberations, including in relation to mediation and article 32 (the "hotchpot" rule) of the Model Law on Cross-Border Insolvency. The Working Group had not yet discussed those issues. More broadly, the Working Group had yet to agree on the appropriate level of flexibility in the draft text. It also needed to decide how to deal with deviations from recommendations 31 to 34 of the *UNCITRAL Legislative Guide on Insolvency Law* (2004)[43] that might result from its current work, as well as how to treat substantive insolvency matters that had repeatedly arisen in its deliberations (e.g. the need for a substantive norm in the text on the stay of arbitral proceedings following the commencement of insolvency proceedings, applicable in both the originating and receiving States).

184. The Commission was informed of the Working Group's request to the secretariat to prepare a revised text in the form of a stand-alone model law. It noted that it had been suggested in the Working Group that it could be decided at a later stage whether any part of a model law should be converted into a different or additional instrument (e.g. amendments to recommendations 31–34 of the Legislative Guide or a supplement to Model Law on Cross-Border Insolvency similar to article X adopted alongside the UNCITRAL Model Law on Recognition and Enforcement of Insolvency-Related Judgments (2018)[44]).

185. The Commission took note of the progress report of Working Group V and requested the Working Group to expedite the finalization of its work on the topic of applicable law in insolvency proceedings.

# XIV. Negotiable cargo documents: progress report of Working Group VI

186. The Commission noted a request by Working Group VI for the secretariat to prepare an explanatory note on the convention on negotiable cargo documents for consideration at its next session (A/CN.9/1205, para. 107).

187. Recalling that several matters raised during the current session and during previous deliberations within the Working Group were to be clarified in the explanatory note, the Commission requested the secretariat to prepare a draft explanatory note on the convention for consideration by Working Group VI at its forty-seventh session, in 2025. Noting that it should not serve as an official commentary on the convention, the Commission authorized the secretariat to publish the revised text of the explanatory note as a document prepared by the secretariat for information purposes, in the six official languages of the United Nations, in both electronic and printed form, and to circulate it widely, along with the text of the convention.

---

[43] United Nations publication, Sales No. E.05.V.10. Available at https://uncitral.un.org/en/texts/insolvency/legislativeguides/insolvency_law.

[44] *Official Records of the General Assembly, Seventy-third Session, Supplement No. 17* (A/73/17), annex III.

# XV. Operationalization of the Advisory Centre on International Investment Dispute Resolution

## A. Introduction

188. The Commission recalled that at its fifty-seventh session, it had adopted the Statute of the Advisory Centre on International Investment Dispute Resolution in principle and had agreed that the operationalization of the Advisory Centre would require further preparatory work to address a number of issues. The Commission had also agreed that in order to facilitate the preparatory work, it would utilize an informal process involving all States and regional economic integration organizations.[45]

189. The Commission noted the progress made at the first meeting on the operationalization of the Advisory Centre, held in Bangkok from 2 to 4 December 2024,[46] and at the second meeting, held in Yerevan from 6 to 8 May 2025.[47] The Commission welcomed the proposal by the Government of France to host the third meeting on the operationalization of the Advisory Centre in Paris from 1 to 3 December 2025.

## B. Comments on the summary of the second meeting on the operationalization of the Advisory Centre

190. The Commission took note of a number of comments, as set forth below, with regard to the summary of the second meeting on the operationalization of the Advisory Centre on International Investment Dispute Resolution as contained in document A/CN.9/1218.

191. It was stated that references to the establishment of the Advisory Centre not having any impact on the budget of the United Nations should be understood broadly to mean that it should not have any impact on the resources of the United Nations, including both the financial and human resources of the secretariat.

192. The view was expressed that the desirability of a two-step process, in which the Centre was first established within the United Nations system as a related organization and subsequently became a specialized agency, was questionable, particularly in respect of the process and budgetary implications. In response, it was noted that there might be benefits in the Advisory Centre becoming a specialized agency and that the matter deserved further consideration. With regard to the budget of the Advisory Centre, it was suggested that the contingency reserve should be increased from 5 to 15 per cent of the overall budget and that the anticipated budget of the Centre should be $4.5 million, plus a contingency reserve of 15 per cent. In response, it was explained that the $4.5 million was a notional figure that the participants at the second meeting on the operationalization of the Advisory Centre had agreed upon, which took into account the need for a contingency reserve.

193. With respect to financing, the view was expressed that membership dues should cover the entirety of the Centre's budget during its initial years of operation. It was suggested that the issue would need to be considered in conjunction with the threshold for entry into force of the Statute. In that context, it was further suggested that voluntary contributions received prior to the entry into force of the Statute should also be taken into account as a separate condition for entry into force. It was suggested that such contributions could be used to fund the operation of the interim secretariat and potentially be credited against future dues.

194. It was noted that at the meetings on the operationalization of the Centre, there had been discussions on decoupling the classification of members for the purposes of

[45] Ibid., *Seventy-ninth Session, Supplement No. 17* (A/79/17), paras. 21, 157–159 and 167.
[46] See A/CN.9/WG.III/WP.251.
[47] See A/CN.9/1218.

determining priority from the classification of members for the purposes of allocating the budget of the Centre. The view was expressed that the existing classification did not fully reflect the objectives of the Centre or global economic realities. It was suggested that the secretariat could prepare two options for classifying members for the purpose of determining the priority to be given to them in accessing services – one based on a decoupled approach, with least developed countries in one category and all other countries in another category, and the other based on three categories of members tailored specifically to the Advisory Centre. It was further stated that the final indicative list for determining priority should form part of the Statute.

## C. Way forward

195. The Commission discussed the way forward to operationalize the Advisory Centre on the basis of the recommendations emanating from the second meeting on the Centre's operationalization.[48] In that context, it was reiterated that as an informal process, the objective of the meetings on the operationalization of the Advisory Centre should be to discuss the various issues but not to take decisions. It was confirmed that in any case, decisions would be taken by the Commission.

196. Views diverged on whether it was appropriate for the Commission to take any decisions at the current session. One view was that because a number of issues remained unresolved, it would be premature and potentially counterproductive for the Commission to take decisions prior to the completion of the operationalization process; flexibility should be preserved so that the Commission had the option of revisiting those issues. Another view was that the taking of decisions by the Commission could expedite the operationalization process as it would enable deliberations to proceed on the basis of those decisions and prevent the reopening of previously discussed matters, without precluding the Commission from revisiting substantive issues if necessary.

197. With regard to the final call for Governments to express their interest in hosting the headquarters or a regional office of the Advisory Centre, the Commission agreed to invite interested Governments to submit to the secretariat a detailed proposal (including financial commitments) by 20 October 2025. It was clarified that the deadline applied equally to those Governments that wished to host the headquarters and those that wished to host the regional offices, as the information provided by the candidate States could inform the Commission on the approach to be taken with regard to the location(s) of the Advisory Centre (see para. 202 below). It was noted that the proposals should include the information listed in paragraph 22 of document A/CN.9/1218 and indicate the financial commitments, which could include both financial and in-kind contributions, to be made by the Government, including premises and any possible support for the interim secretariat. The possibility of Governments' presenting joint proposals was also mentioned. However, it was noted that States would not be precluded from indicating their willingness to host a regional office once the Advisory Centre had been established.

198. The Commission also invited interested Governments to make an oral presentation at the third meeting on the operationalization of the Advisory Centre and requested that recordings of the presentations be made available to the Commission next year.

199. The Government of Morocco expressed its interest in hosting the Advisory Centre. Other Governments that had previously expressed their interest reiterated their continued interest.

200. With regard to the relationship of the Advisory Centre to the United Nations, the Commission recognized that the meetings on the operationalization of the Centre would proceed on the basis that the Advisory Centre should aim to become a related

[48] See A/CN.9/1218, paras. 53–61.

organization of the United Nations, and requested that work be undertaken by the interim secretariat of the Centre on the terms of a possible relationship agreement based on existing agreements concluded between the United Nations and related organizations. It was noted that that would not rule out the possibility of the Advisory Centre becoming a specialized agency of the United Nations at a later stage.

201. With regard to the location of the Advisory Centre, the Commission acknowledged that the meetings on the operationalization of the Advisory Centre would proceed on the basis that the location of the Advisory Centre would be determined taking a holistic approach to the following factors: support from the host State/Government; a stable environment; accessibility and affordability; geographical distribution; attractiveness to a qualified workforce; and cooperation and coordination. That list of factors was not exhaustive, and the factors should be understood broadly, as discussed at the second meeting on the operationalization of the Advisory Centre.

202. It was noted that pursuant to article 9, paragraph 2, of the Statute, only the location of the headquarters was to be identified, and that the Commission, in adopting the Statute in principle, had decided that a decision regarding the existence and location of regional offices was better left to the Governing Committee of the Advisory Centre. However, preference was expressed for indicating the number and locations of the regional offices in the Statute. It was noted that during the operationalization process, it had become clear that identifying the regional offices in the Statute could highlight the Centre's accessibility and inclusiveness, and the Commission should conduct a full analysis of where the Centre should have a presence. However, the view was also expressed that regional offices should be established after the headquarters, given the related resource implications. It was further noted that the meetings on the operationalization of the centre should be aimed at identifying criteria for selecting the location(s) rather than at making decisions in that regard.

203. The Commission further requested the secretariat to explore possible means for it to function as the interim secretariat of the Advisory Centre once the Statute had been finalized and adopted by the General Assembly, without any budget implications for the United Nations and without detriment to the provision by the secretariat of services to the Commission as a whole. The secretariat was also requested to consider other alternatives.

204. The Commission agreed that the preparatory work should continue to be based on the Statute as adopted in principle, and that the third and any subsequent meetings on the operationalization of the Advisory Centre should focus on the following issues: (a) privileges and immunities of the Advisory Centre and its staff members; (b) mechanisms to ensure sustainable operations, with an anticipated notional budget of approximately $4.5 million; (c) modalities for determining the amount of contributions by members based on the scale of assessments of the United Nations, and methods of payment; (d) the classification of members to determine the priority to be given to them in accessing the services of the Centre, delinked to the contribution to be made by members; (e) thresholds for membership and financial contributions for the entry into force of the Statute; (f) the anticipated mandate and functions of the interim secretariat; (g) the location(s) of the Advisory Centre; and (h) any necessary amendments to the Statute.

205. It was further agreed that, based on the outcome of the meetings on the operationalization of the Advisory Centre, the Commission would aim to finalize the Statute at its fifty-ninth session and present it to the General Assembly. To achieve that goal, the Commission encouraged participants in the third meeting on the operationalization of the Advisory Centre in Paris to comprehensively discuss the issues outlined in the previous paragraph.

206. The Commission discussed how the outcome of the meetings on the operationalization of the Advisory Centre should be reported to the Commission. The diverging views expressed at the previous session of the Commission (see A/79/17,

para. 160) were reiterated. It was recalled that the Commission had agreed that the results of the first meeting on the operationalization of the Advisory Centre could be made available to Working Group III for an exchange of views, as there was additional conference time available for that purpose.

207. One view was that the summary of the third and any subsequent meetings on the operationalization of the Advisory Centre should be reported to Working Group III to ensure a more transparent and inclusive process and allow for in-depth deliberations. Accordingly, it was proposed that some conference time be allocated for that purpose at a subsequent session of Working Group III. Another view was that the Working Group had completed its deliberations on the Statute and that its operationalization was an ad hoc process initiated by the Commission. It was said that as the authority to take decisions remained with the Commission, there would not be much merit in reporting back to the Working Group.

208. In addition, it was suggested that there should be a process for allowing participants in a meeting on the operationalization of the Advisory Centre to comment on the summary before it was presented to the Commission and that after its issuance, the summary could be circulated more broadly for comments. It was further suggested that informal meetings could be held, including on the margins of a Working Group session, to provide information about the process.

209. A question was raised with regard to the role of observer States and organizations when the Commission took decisions.

210. After discussion, it was agreed that the operationalization process for the Advisory Centre should be as follows:

(a) The summary of a meeting on the operationalization of the Advisory Centre would be subject to a written consultation process among the participants in that meeting. Once finalized, the summary would be circulated for further comment by Commission and Working Group III delegations. The summary, along with any comments received, would then be presented at the next session of the Commission;

(b) The secretariat would be requested to reflect on the range of issues raised and to prepare a revised version of the Statute as appropriate and present it, along with other issues pertaining to the operationalization of the Advisory Centre, to the Commission at its next session, so that the Commission could take informed decisions to finalize the Statute and operationalize the Centre;

(c) Side events could be held at sessions of Working Group III to provide delegates with information about the operationalization of the Advisory Centre and to gather additional perspectives. The secretariat would be asked to consider holding additional informal meetings on the operationalization of the Advisory Centre.

211. The Commission reiterated its request to the secretariat to continue to provide support for the meetings on the operationalization of the Advisory Centre, including the preparation of background documents and the provision of partial travel support to participants from developing countries, subject to available resources. The Commission also requested the secretariat to continue to consult with Governments that had expressed an interest in hosting additional meetings on the operationalization of the Advisory Centre.

# XVI. Work programme

## A. Legislative programme under consideration by working groups

212. The Commission noted the progress of its working groups as reported at the session (see chaps. X–XIV of the present report) and reaffirmed the programme of

current legislative activities set out in table 1 of document A/CN.9/1210, supplemented as follows:

(a) The Commission authorized the secretariat to utilize the conference resources tentatively allocated to Working Group I in the second half of 2025 and the first half of 2026, as well as any conference resources of other working groups that might become available, to hold colloquiums on various topics (see para. 347 below);

(b) With respect to dispute settlement, Working Group II should continue to work on the recognition and enforcement of electronic arbitral awards and, subsequently, on electronic notices;

(c) With respect to investor-State dispute settlement reform, Working Group III should continue with its work programme as mandated;

(d) With respect to electronic commerce, Working Group IV should continue to work on the formulation of default rules on data provision contracts;

(e) With respect to insolvency law, Working Group V should continue its work on the topic of applicable law in insolvency proceedings and review the updated draft of the *UNCITRAL Practice Guide on Cross-Border Insolvency Cooperation*[49] being prepared by the secretariat;

(f) With respect to negotiable cargo documents, Working Group VI should review the explanatory note on the draft convention on negotiable cargo documents to be prepared by the secretariat (see para. 187 above).

## B. Additional topics considered at earlier sessions of the Commission

### 1. Climate change mitigation, adaptation and resilience

213. The Commission recalled that, at its fifty-fourth session, it had heard a proposal to examine how existing UNCITRAL texts could be aligned with climate change mitigation, adaptation and resilience goals and whether future work could be done by UNCITRAL to facilitate those goals in the implementation of those texts or through the development of new texts.[50] The Commission further recalled that, at its fifty-seventh session, it had requested the secretariat to organize a two-day colloquium with a focus on the relevance of UNCITRAL texts to climate action.[51] The Commission noted that the UNCITRAL Colloquium on the Law of International Trade for a Greener Future had been held in Vienna on 23 and 24 October 2024. Participants had considered how UNCITRAL texts related to and could support climate change mitigation, adaptation and resilience goals in the areas of public procurement, the international sale of goods, public-private partnerships and dispute settlement.

214. The Commission had before it the following three notes by the secretariat: (a) the report on the Colloquium, which reflected the panels' discussions and contained a list of recommendations and findings, with a view to strengthening existing UNCITRAL texts or developing new UNCITRAL texts for a greener future (A/CN.9/1204); (b) the work programme of the Commission, which complemented the report on the Colloquium (A/CN.9/1210, paras. 11–14); and (c) a note on possible future work in the area of public procurement, which discussed the scope of such work (A/CN.9/1230). The Commission also had before it a proposal by Viet Nam for possible future work on carbon markets (A/CN.9/1231).

[49] United Nations publication, Sales No E.10.V.6.

[50] *Official Records of the General Assembly, Seventy-sixth Session, Supplement No. 17* (A/76/17), paras. 244–246.

[51] Ibid., *Seventy-ninth Session, Supplement No. 17* (A/79/17), para. 276.

### (a) Public procurement

215. At the outset, the view was reiterated that climate-related issues fell outside the mandate of UNCITRAL and that those issues were already being considered in other forums (see para. 253 below). It was noted that it could be challenging to reach consensus on sensitive issues relevant to domestic policy choices and to reconcile different understandings of what "green" procurement was intended to mean and what it was supposed to cover.

216. However, it was stated that environmental and sustainability considerations merited further examination to ensure that the Model Law on Public Procurement[52] and related texts would be fully up to date and provide appropriate guidance to States to strengthen their public procurement regimes. Ongoing discussions relevant to the Model Law in other forums (e.g. the sustainable procurement work programme under the Agreement on Government Procurement of the World Trade Organization (WTO)) and the need to ensure consistent approaches at the global level were also mentioned as justifying work on the topic. In that context, it was stressed that environmental or sustainability requirements should not lead to unjust discrimination by procuring entities, in line with the provisions of the Agreement on Government Procurement.

217. With respect to topics that were listed as potentially deserving attention as part of a possible update of the Model Law, suspension and debarment, as well as recent developments in the area of e-procurement, were considered relevant and timely. Doubts were expressed about extending the scope of the procurement cycle covered in the Model Law to the planning phase. The recommendation emanating from the UNCITRAL Colloquium on the Law of International Trade for a Greener Future to develop a new legal instrument promoting cross-border trade as a tool for decarbonization and green procurement policies did not receive support.

218. It was generally felt that embarking on work to update the Model Law in order to support the "greening" of public procurement was not desirable. However, support was expressed for updating the Model Law to reflect recent developments in other areas, including e-procurement and the work being undertaken by other international organizations, such as WTO and its Committee on Government Procurement, OECD and the World Bank.

219. After discussion, the Commission requested the secretariat to conduct preparatory work, in coordination with relevant international organizations such as WTO, OECD and the World Bank, to refine the scope of possible work on updating the Model Law and related texts to reflect recent developments, which would not include issues of climate change mitigation, adaptation and resilience, and to report back to the Commission at its fifty-ninth session.

### (b) Other areas considered at the UNCITRAL Colloquium on the Law of International Trade for a Greener Future

220. The Commission took note of the conclusions related to the United Nations Sales Convention (1980) and dispute settlement reached at the Colloquium (A/CN.9/1204, para. 32). With respect to the conclusions relating to the Convention in particular, the view was expressed that work in that regard would need to be sufficiently inclusive to address the concern of many States, in particular developing States, that imposing environmental requirements along the supply chain and the contractual cycle might create additional burdens for them and their businesses to take part in international trade.

221. The Commission considered a proposal by UNIDROIT to cooperate and undertake joint work on the development of a legal guide on corporate sustainability due diligence in global value chains. The Commission was informed that the project, which was a high priority for UNIDROIT, was focused on private law aspects, in particular the legal regime for the contractualization of sustainable standards along

[52] Ibid., *Sixty-sixth Session, Supplement No. 17* (A/66/17), annex I.

the supply chain (e.g. remedies available in the event of the breach of an obligation) and was not intended to address the substance of the sustainability standards.

222. The Commission expressed its appreciation to UNIDROIT for seeking the involvement of UNCITRAL in the project. However, recalling the discussions held at the UNCITRAL Colloquium on Climate Change and International Trade Law (Vienna, 12 and 13 July 2023) on advancing climate-responsible corporate conduct and adaptation strategies and approaches available to private sector operators to promote sustainability in their supply chains,[53] the Commission decided not to embark on the project but requested that it be informed of any developments.

### (c) Carbon markets

223. It was explained that the proposal by Viet Nam for possible future work on carbon markets envisaged the conduct by the secretariat of further exploratory work to take stock of initiatives currently being undertaken by various international organizations and in other forums, to review developments with respect to bilateral agreements being concluded under article 6 of the Paris Agreement and to examine domestic legislation, as well as case law, on carbon markets, in order to identify gaps in legal frameworks and obstacles to the cross-border trading of carbon credits. It was further explained that the work could be aimed at identifying best practices and models for States seeking to develop and enhance their domestic legal frameworks to support carbon markets and facilitate cross-border trading of carbon credits.

224. Support was expressed for the proposal, because the trading of carbon credits, as a matter of international trade, fell squarely within the mandate of UNCITRAL and because work in the area could support the development of domestic legal frameworks to enable and facilitate cross-border trading of carbon credits. The work would be particularly beneficial for developing countries in need of such support. It was further pointed out that a stocktaking exercise to map out the various initiatives and recent developments at the international and domestic levels could identify legal gaps, which would allow the Commission to make a more informed decision at its next session. It was noted that a more refined proposal could be presented to the Commission at a later stage.

225. However, concern was expressed that work in the area could overlap with work being undertaken in other forums and might be better addressed in such forums, for example, meetings held within the framework of the United Nations Framework Convention on Climate Change. The view was also expressed that the proposal was not specific enough and work in that area might be premature. Lastly, given the scarcity of resources of the Commission and its secretariat, it was stated that caution should be exercised with respect to such work.

226. While expressing its appreciation to the Government of Viet Nam for the proposal, the Commission agreed not to take up work related to carbon markets at that time.

## 2. Secured transactions using new types of assets and their treatment under the UNCITRAL Model Law on Secured Transactions (2016)

227. The Commission recalled that, at its fifty-seventh session, it had requested the secretariat to take stock of legislative developments related to new types of assets to examine how the Model Law on Secured Transactions[54] had been implemented, and to organize a colloquium involving experts and representatives of international and

[53] Ibid., *Seventy-eighth Session, Supplement No. 17* (A/78/17), paras. 191 and 192.

[54] General Assembly resolution 71/136, annex.

regional organizations to clarify and refine various aspects of possible future work in the area.[55]

228. The Commission had before it the report on the colloquium on secured transactions, on the theme of "Navigating the new era of digital finance – UNCITRAL Model Law on Secured Transactions and the use of new types of assets for secured financing" (A/CN.9/1201), held in New York on 20 and 21 February 2025, which was supplemented by a list of issues identified by the secretariat in relation to possible future work. Those issues included definitions and characterizations of new types of assets (including whether they would fall within the scope of the Model Law), the creation of security rights in such assets, means to achieve third-party effectiveness, priority among competing security rights, rights and obligations of the parties and third-party obligors, enforcement and conflict-of-law rules (see A/CN.9/1210, paras. 15–28).

229. The Commission noted that the Colloquium had provided a valuable opportunity to take stock of the recent developments with regard to State legislation, the use of new types of assets as collateral, new financing techniques, as well as work undertaken or being undertaken by other international organizations. It was emphasized that any future work in the area should be closely coordinated with work by other organizations to avoid overlap and ensure consistency. Reference was made to the UNIDROIT Principles on Digital Assets and Private Law, as well as the Digital Tokens Project of HCCH.

230. While the view was expressed that the Model Law already sufficiently addressed the issues identified in document A/CN.9/1210, it was widely felt that the secretariat should be tasked with exploratory work to identify concrete gaps that required updates to the Model Law or other texts on secured transactions, prior to any work being undertaken by a working group. In support, it was said that such a stocktaking exercise could further assist States implementing secured transactions reforms on the basis of the Model Law. It was suggested that a colloquium or an expert group meeting could be organized for that purpose.

231. After discussion, the Commission instructed the secretariat to continue to monitor developments in the area, in particular those of other international organizations, and as part of its preparatory work, to convene an expert group meeting or a colloquium involving representatives of relevant international organizations to define the scope and form of any future work and to report back to the Commission in 2026.

### 3. Dispute resolution in the digital economy

232. The Commission recalled that, at its fifty-seventh session, it had requested the secretariat to continue to implement the project on the stocktaking of developments in dispute resolution in the digital economy, endorsed at its fifty-fourth session and funded by the Government of Japan, to further monitor and explore relevant topics such as those related to artificial intelligence and platform-based dispute resolution, in collaboration with the Inclusive Global Legal Innovation Platform on Online Dispute Resolution.[56]

233. At the current session, the Commission had before it a note by the secretariat containing a progress report on the stocktaking of developments in dispute resolution in the digital economy (A/CN.9/1215), which contained a summary of the progress made in the exploratory work on the topic of the use of artificial intelligence in dispute resolution, and a submission from the Inclusive Global Legal Innovation Platform on Online Dispute Resolution (A/CN.9/1224), which contained a summary of the progress made in the work carried out by the Platform on the topic of platform-based dispute resolution. The Commission also had before it a submission from the

[55] *Official Records of the General Assembly, Seventy-ninth Session, Supplement No. 17* (A/79/17), para. 295.

[56] Ibid., para. 284.

Government of Israel regarding exploratory work on remote arbitration and mediation (A/CN.9/1233).

234. Broad support was expressed for the secretariat to continue its monitoring and exploratory work on the use of artificial intelligence in dispute resolution. The view was expressed that a proactive approach by the Commission was needed to address the impact of artificial intelligence on fundamental principles such as due process and fairness, and to ensure legal certainty and transparency, particularly to avoid situations in which the use of artificial intelligence could result in the enforcement of awards being refused under the Convention on the Recognition and Enforcement of Foreign Arbitral Awards (1958 New York Convention).[57] The view was also expressed that some of the issues identified were suitable for consideration by a working group, on the understanding that the relevant use cases and legal issues to be addressed should be further specified. Conversely, a general note of caution was sounded that any future work would need to be carefully thought out in view of the sensitive nature of issues related to the use of artificial intelligence, and to ensure that the work remained relevant over time, particularly given the rapid pace of technological advancement.

235. With regard to the proposal to undertake work on standards for platform-based dispute resolution, it was recalled that the Commission had adopted the Technical Notes on Online Dispute Resolution in 2016, and the rationale for undertaking further work was not clear, particularly as difficulties in achieving consensus remained unresolved and ways to overcome them had not been explored sufficiently. On the other hand, the need to prepare harmonized standards to ensure the legitimacy of such processes, especially in light of the recent developments in the digital economy, was emphasized. It was stressed that issues relating to consumer protection should be avoided. The need to clarify the contractual relationships among stakeholders was highlighted, and it was suggested that the inclusion of new or revised standards – such as those addressing suitability – could be beneficial.

236. Broad support was expressed for the conduct of further exploratory work on the development of procedural guidance regarding key aspects of remote hearings in arbitration and the conduct of mediation, which offered a flexible, efficient and cost-effective alternative to in-person proceedings. It was noted that the stocktaking of institutional practices, including a comparative analysis, would be useful, and references were made to relevant instruments, such as the Convention on the Taking of Evidence Abroad in Civil or Commercial Matters. It was emphasized that the scope of any procedural guidance should be carefully defined, taking into account the 1958 New York Convention. It was further observed that the use of digital platforms for holding such hearings should be considered in that context.

237. After discussion, the Commission noted with appreciation the proposals and the work carried out by the secretariat. Appreciation was also expressed to the Government of Japan for its continued support of the project on dispute resolution in the digital economy. The Commission requested the secretariat to continue its exploratory work on the project, in particular: (a) the use of artificial intelligence in dispute resolution; (b) platform-based dispute resolution, in collaboration with the Inclusive Global Legal Innovation Platform on Online Dispute Resolution; and (c) the development of procedural guidance on remote hearings in arbitration and the conduct of mediation. It requested the secretariat to report on progress made at the fifty-ninth session. The Commission also requested that a questionnaire be circulated to States for further input on the aforementioned topics. The Commission further requested that a colloquium be held during a session of Working Group II regarding topics (a) and (c), to enable the Working Group to formulate a recommendation to the Commission on possible future work.

[57] United Nations, *Treaty Series*, vol. 330, No. 4739, p. 3.

### 4. Electronic commerce and paperless trade

238. The Commission had before it a note by the Secretariat on the stocktaking of UNCITRAL texts that referred to electronic aspects (A/CN.9/1226). It was recalled that the note had been prepared in response to a request by the Commission (A/79/17, para. 299).

239. It was indicated that the note also contained a discussion of UNCITRAL texts and paperless trade aimed at assisting the Commission in deciding on the next steps regarding the contribution of UNCITRAL texts to such trade. The Commission also had before it a note by the Russian Federation on possible future work on legal aspects of paperless trade (A/CN.9/1234).

240. Broad support was expressed for pursuing that stocktaking exercise and for encouraging further submissions by States on their uptake of UNCITRAL texts. It was indicated that the exercise highlighted the positive impact of UNCITRAL texts on the development of electronic commerce and the way they supported the development of digital trade by facilitating the transition from paper to electronic form, as well as with respect to the use of data and new technologies.

241. The view was expressed that the exercise was fundamental for not only mapping existing texts and ensuring their coherent application but also identifying any legislative gaps. The ongoing work of HCCH to complement article 19 of the Model Law on Electronic Transferable Records with private international law rules was mentioned as being complementary to the stocktaking exercise and as showcasing seamless cooperation among organizations. The results of a study on the implementation of UNCITRAL and other texts on electronic commerce were shared (A/CN.9/1234, para. 8). It was indicated that attention should be paid to ensuring consistency with the core texts and that the work would benefit from focusing on discrete issues rather than an all-encompassing approach. It was also said that the views and needs of developing and least developed countries would need to be taken into account in the exercise.

242. Noting the utility of the stocktaking exercise, the Commission requested the secretariat to continue to compile and start to consolidate UNCITRAL texts on electronic commerce into a single legislative text, including by preparing guidance material on their consistent implementation, and to submit the outcome to a working group for review at a later stage.

243. Broad support was also expressed for continuing the exploratory work on legal aspects of paperless trade with a view to preparing guidance materials or even model legislation. Examples were provided of close cooperation with other entities, including the Economic and Social Commission for Asia and the Pacific. The close interaction of UNCITRAL texts with other texts, such as the Framework Agreement on Facilitation of Cross-border Paperless Trade in Asia and the Pacific, was also highlighted. It was noted that several States Parties to the Framework Agreement had adopted the United Nations Convention on the Use of Electronic Communications in International Contracts (2005), and that the two instruments were complementary. It was suggested that a pilot project on paperless trade could be set up for States in Central America under the auspices of the Secretariat for Central American Economic Integration.

244. The desirability of providing guidance on cross-border recognition of the effect of application of trust services and on implementation of the concept of "substantially equivalent level of reliability" was noted. The desirability of holding a colloquium to further discuss relevant issues was also noted. The view was expressed that procedures for the submission of electronic documents to public entities such as customs authorities touched upon regulatory matters, which were outside the scope of the projected work.

245. After discussion, the Commission requested the secretariat to continue its preparatory work on enabling end-to-end trade digitalization and paperless trade,

emphasizing a step-by-step approach to the work. In that regard, it was agreed that a colloquium could be held to explore the use of UNCITRAL texts on electronic commerce for paperless trade with a view to presenting guidance text and possible model legislation on paperless trade to the Commission for consideration at its next session.

## C. Additional topics considered at the current session

246. The Commission recalled its role in deliberating on the desirability and prioritization of future work in any area of international trade law and on modalities for undertaking such work – whether it was carried out by the Commission itself, its working groups or the secretariat – and on whether a colloquium or other expert consultations would be necessary before any particular topic was referred to a working group. It also recalled the criteria that it had formulated as a basis for any decisions in that regard.[58]

### 1. Possible future work in the area of insolvency law

247. For its consideration of the sub-item on possible future work in the area of insolvency law, the Commission had before it: (a) a proposal by the delegation of Australia on the preparation of an update to the Guide to Enactment and Interpretation of the UNCITRAL Model Law on Cross-Border Insolvency, that proposal originally having been submitted to Working Group V at its sixty-fifth session (A/CN.9/WG.V/WP.199);[59] (b) a submission by the Government of France on possible future work relating to insolvency, the environment and sustainability (A/CN.9/1232); (c) the report of Working Group V on the work of its sixty-fifth session (Vienna, 16–20 December 2024) (A/CN.9/1198), paragraphs 58 to 62 of which summarized the deliberations of the Working Group on the proposals received at that session regarding possible future work by UNCITRAL in the area of insolvency law; and (d) a note by the Secretariat on possible future work in the area of insolvency law (A/CN.9/1219).

248. In that context, the Commission recalled that the Working Group had finalized its work on the topic of asset tracing and recovery in insolvency proceedings and had continued to work on the topic of applicable law in insolvency proceedings (see chaps. V and XIII of the present report). It also recalled that the Working Group was expected to review an updated version of the *UNCITRAL Practice Guide on Cross-Border Insolvency Cooperation* prior to its transmission to the Commission for consideration and finalization.[60] The Commission noted the progress made by the secretariat in preparing that update and the indicative timeline for its completion (2026–2027), which would depend on the availability of secretariat resources and the workload of Working Group V. The Commission was also informed that the timeline for the completion by the Working Group of its work on the topic of applicable law in insolvency proceedings might be relevant for the completion of updates to the *Practice Guide*, since it would be desirable to reflect the outcomes of that work in those updates. In that regard, the Commission noted the secretariat's plans to incorporate the results of the work by UNCITRAL on asset tracing and recovery in insolvency proceedings into the updated *Practice Guide*, including by annexing the UNCITRAL Toolkit on Expedited Asset Tracing and Recovery in Insolvency Proceedings, as adopted by the Commission at the current session (see para. 133 above), to that publication.

---

[58] Ibid., *Sixty-eighth Session, Supplement No. 17* (A/68/17), paras. 303–307.

[59] A/CN.9/1198, para. 58.

[60] *Official Records of the General Assembly, Seventy-ninth Session, Supplement No. 17* (A/79/17), para. 256.

### (a) Update of the Guide to Enactment and Interpretation of the UNCITRAL Model Law on Cross-Border Insolvency

249. Broad support was expressed for the proposal to update the Guide to Enactment and Interpretation of the UNCITRAL Model Law on Cross-Border Insolvency, of 2013. However, views differed on whether that work should be assigned to Working Group V. The view was expressed that the secretariat, in consultation with experts, could prepare the update, which could subsequently be reviewed by the Working Group. It was suggested that a colloquium should be held to delineate the scope of the expected updates to the Guide, after which the Commission would be in a position to decide whether to allocate the work to the Working Group or the secretariat.

250. After discussion, the Commission agreed that updating the Guide would be both timely and necessary in light of the significant jurisprudence relating to the Model Law that had emerged since 2013, including from jurisdictions that had enacted the Model Law after 2013, the growing complexity of cases of cross-border insolvency, and the important role that the Guide played in supporting the proper understanding, enactment, use, application and interpretation of the Model Law. The view was expressed that an updated version of the Guide could also provide impetus for the enactment by States of the Model Law and the two subsequent UNCITRAL model laws in the area of insolvency law. The Commission endorsed the proposal to hold a colloquium to discuss the scope of possible updates to the Guide (see paras. 256 and 347 below for consideration of the date, place and format of the colloquium).

### (b) Insolvency, the environment and sustainability

251. The Commission recalled its earlier efforts, including the holding of several colloquiums, to identify the relevance of international trade law to endeavours to combat climate change. Echoing several points raised on those occasions, such as the prerogatives of States and competent United Nations bodies to address matters related to climate change and environmental protection, views differed as to whether the proposal for possible future work relating to insolvency, the environment and sustainability should be taken up by the Commission.

252. One view was that the proposal should be considered only to the extent that it was relevant to the work of UNCITRAL and Working Group V. It was suggested that a colloquium could help identify relevant issues, for example, those not currently addressed in domestic insolvency laws and in other legislation at the intersection of insolvency and other areas of law (e.g. directors' obligations vis-à-vis the environment, or the implementation of the "polluter pays" principle when the polluter was insolvent).

253. Another view was that the Commission should not take up the proposal, including by allocating it for discussion at a colloquium, because, among other reasons, the proposal raised public policy and domestic law issues on which it would currently be impossible to reach consensus at the international level. Further concerns were expressed that the topic involved complex issues of public international law that were being addressed in other United Nations forums (namely, meetings held within the framework of the United Nations Framework Convention on Climate Change and the United Nations Environment Programme), that the topic fell outside the mandate of UNCITRAL, and that its consideration by UNCITRAL could result in the fragmentation of an already complex area of international law. Additionally, the view was expressed that introducing changes to the UNCITRAL insolvency framework through the lens of environmental law and climate change was not advisable, as such changes could conflict with policy choices already embedded in that framework or currently under discussion by the Working Group. Furthermore, doubts were expressed as to whether the issues raised in the proposal were a priority for States in the context of their environmental protection and climate change agendas. The view was expressed that efforts to harmonize the regulation of environmental considerations in insolvency proceedings might impinge on State sovereignty, create new environmental obligations inconsistent with the current cooperative nature of

international environmental law, and shift costs and legal risks to developing countries.

254. After discussion and having noted the concern expressed by some delegations that there had not been sufficient time to consider the proposal properly, the Commission concluded that the proposal was not yet ripe for discussion by UNCITRAL. The delegation that had made the proposal was invited to develop it with a view to making it more relevant in practical and concrete terms to the UNCITRAL mandate and insolvency law framework and the expertise in Working Group V.

#### (c) Other topics

255. With regard to other topics for possible future work in the area of insolvency law, as listed in a note by the Secretariat (A/CN.9/1219), the Commission heard that a colloquium could address, alongside updates to the Guide to Enactment and Interpretation of the UNCITRAL Model Law on Cross-Border Insolvency (see para. 250 above), financial contracts, with a view to updating the relevant section of the Legislative Guide on Insolvency Law, as well as creditor claims and third-party releases in cross-border insolvency, but considerations arising from the use of artificial intelligence in insolvency proceedings should be excluded from the colloquium's scope. Views differed on whether issues arising from informal debt restructuring proceedings would be worth pursuing by UNCITRAL.

#### (d) Next steps

256. The Commission agreed to consider the dates and venue for a colloquium on possible future work in the area of insolvency law later in the session (for the subsequent discussion of those matters, see para. 347 below). It was suggested that the colloquium could be held for two days in conjunction with the next session of Working Group V, with efforts made to provide for online participation.

### 2. Legal issues relating to the use of decentralized autonomous organizations in trade

257. The Commission had before it a note on legal issues relating to the use of decentralized autonomous organizations in trade (A/CN.9/1225). It was explained that decentralized autonomous organizations were a specific type of computer code used to manage distributed ledgers and, as organizational entities used to offer commercial and non-commercial services, possessed a governance structure, based on distributed ledger technology, that relied on the use of token-based voting and smart contracts for decision-making, and lacked centralized management.

258. It was added that, during finalization of the guidance document on legal issues arising from the use of distributed ledger technology, it was felt that the legal treatment of decentralized autonomous organizations raised novel issues that were addressed in a piecemeal manner by the emerging legal framework. For instance, it was noted that existing case law dealt with liability for the loss of control of digital assets and the treatment of decentralized autonomous organizations in insolvency proceedings. However, the law did not comprehensively address other important matters, such as the legal personality of decentralized autonomous organizations and the separation of assets between decentralized autonomous organizations and their participants.

259. For that reason, it was indicated that it might be useful to, on the one hand, include explanatory content on decentralized autonomous organizations in the guidance document on legal issues arising from the use of distributed ledger technology and to, on the other hand, consider whether the use of decentralized autonomous organizations could benefit from a comprehensive and uniform legal framework. Accordingly, it was suggested that the Commission might wish to consider whether exploratory work on legal issues relating to decentralized autonomous organizations should be carried

out by the secretariat with a view to the Commission considering possible future legislative work in the area at its fifty-ninth session.

260. Broad support was expressed for conducting exploratory work on decentralized autonomous organizations. It was indicated that such organizations were at the intersection of artificial intelligence, distributed ledger technology and company law, and that international dialogue was needed from an early stage of their use to promote global interoperability and avoid legal fragmentation. The importance of achieving legal clarity in the area was also highlighted, and it was suggested that work could be carried out in cooperation with other relevant international organizations. It was noted that decentralized autonomous organizations were already being used for several purposes and their features were being considered in various States.

261. The Commission took note with appreciation of the content of document A/CN.9/1225 and requested the secretariat to monitor developments on legal issues relating to the use of decentralized autonomous organizations in trade, to carry out further exploratory work, including in cooperation with HCCH and within available resources, and to report back to the Commission on that work at a future session.

### 3. Legal aspects of digital trade

262. The Commission had before it a note by the Secretariat containing a proposal by the United Arab Emirates and Spain for possible future work on legal aspects of digital trade, with a special focus on digital platforms (A/CN.9/1227). The Commission heard that the proposal drew connections with exploratory work carried out by the secretariat in response to a request by the Commission, at its fifty-first session, in 2018, to compile information on legal issues related to the digital economy.[61] It was recalled that the exploratory work was focused on five topics (namely, artificial intelligence, data, digital assets, online platforms and distributed ledger systems) and had so far resulted in the publication of the *Taxonomy of Legal Issues Related to the Digital Economy*[62] and the development of proposals on the use of artificial intelligence and automation in contracting and on data provision contracts, which the Commission had referred to Working Group IV at its fifty-fifth session.[63] It was also recalled that the secretariat had previously reported to the Commission on possible future work on the topic of online platforms based on its exploratory work (A/CN.9/1064, paras. 10–14 and 25).

263. The Commission heard that digital platforms were a defining feature of the digital economy. It was recalled that the proposal had been presented to Working Group IV at its the sixty-seventh session, where it had prompted the exchange of views about possible future work on the topic (see para. 179 above). The view that digital trade comprised both new means of trading and new items being traded was reiterated (A/CN.9/1197, para. 74), and it was added that platform operators represented a new type of actor in trade. It was observed that platform operators served not only as intermediaries, but also as architects of online marketplaces for trading, which in turn were governed by platform rules.

264. It was stressed that, while certain digital platforms were subject to regulatory regimes, the operation of digital platforms fundamentally relied on contracts, notably the contract between platform operator and user and the contract between platform users, which were concluded through the platform. It was noted that applying existing private law to the operation of digital platforms had raised novel legal issues regarding the characterization of the contract between platform operator and user, the rights and obligations of the parties under that contract, including due diligence, and the availability of contractual remedies to enforce compliance with platform rules,

---

[61] Ibid., *Seventy-third Session, Supplement No. 17* (A/73/17), para. 253 (b).

[62] United Nations publication, Sales No. E.12.V.11.

[63] *Official Records of the General Assembly, Seventy-seventh Session, Supplement No. 17* (A/77/17), paras. 159 and 163.

among others. It was emphasized that the proposal was to explore those issues in more detail to refine the scope of any future work.

265. Broad support was expressed for the proposal and the exploratory work as matters of international trade law. It was suggested that the concept of "digital platform" was broad and that work could focus on online marketplaces. It was also suggested that eventual preparatory work could be guided by the principles of transparency, equity and due diligence. It was added that work towards harmonized legal rules had the potential to promote greater openness and inclusivity in the digital economy, inject greater balance between platform operator and user, and allow for greater system interoperability and integration in global supply chains.

266. After discussion, it was agreed that exploratory work should be conducted, with a focus on digital platforms and private law, including an assessment of the desirability and feasibility of developing a harmonized legal text, possibly in the form of a model law. It was further agreed that a colloquium could be held to consider the legal issues outlined in the proposal and to take stock of relevant legislative responses, which could be reported to the Commission next year. It was emphasized that regulatory issues such as data privacy and protection, consumer protection, intellectual property and competition law should be avoided. The envisaged cooperation with HCCH was welcomed.

### 4. Digital payments

267. The Commission had before it a note by the Secretariat on possible future work in the area of digital payments, supported by Saudi Arabia and Sierra Leone (A/CN.9/1229). It was recalled that UNCITRAL had long worked in the area of payments, including its publication of the *UNCITRAL Legal Guide on Electronic Funds Transfers* (1986)[64] and its adoption of the UNCITRAL Model Law on International Credit Transfers (1992).[65] It was indicated that the note provided background information on developments in payment methods and systems that, along with the development of e-commerce, had led to exponential growth in digital payments around the globe and efforts to facilitate digital trade, including through provisions on digital trade in free trade agreements, digital economy agreements and other similar instruments, and that the exploratory work proposed in the note would take into account those developments and existing initiatives, as well as related frameworks and regulations. It was further indicated that the secretariat could embark on exploratory work involving experts and relevant stakeholders and that the note recommended the holding of a colloquium, the results of which could be reported to the Commission at its fifty-ninth session.

268. Support was expressed for the proposal. It was noted that the work could explore the need to develop an enabling legal framework that reduced complexities, enhanced legal certainty, mutual recognition and interoperability, and promoted affordability, transparency and financial inclusion. It was also noted that digital payments were an important part of digital trade and that the work could build on existing UNCITRAL texts such as the UNCITRAL Model Law on International Credit Transfers (1992) and the UNCITRAL Model Law on the Use and Cross-border Recognition of Identity Management and Trust Services (2022),[66] as well as other initiatives such as the Protocol to the Agreement Establishing the African Continental Free Trade Area on Digital Trade and work at WTO.

269. However, concerns were also expressed. It was noted that payments and payment systems intersected with regulatory regimes, including financial regulations and regulations to counter money-laundering and the financing of terrorism. The need was emphasized to take a cautious approach so as to ensure that the exploratory work

[64] United Nations publication, Sales No. E.87.V.9.

[65] *Official Records of the General Assembly, Forty-seventh Session, Supplement No. 17* (A/47/17), annex I.

[66] Ibid., *Seventy-seventh Session, Supplement No. 17* (A/77/17), annex II.

would clearly define the scope of work and the issues to be addressed. A view was expressed that the topic was overly broad and that the specific issues deserving legislative work should be identified at the outset, and a revised proposal should be submitted. It was said that the exploratory work could bring together experts to consider the private law and international trade law issues and refine the scope, with the outcome of such work being reported to the Commission.

270. After discussion, the Commission welcomed the proposal and requested the secretariat to carry out exploratory work on the topic of digital payments. To that end, it was agreed that a colloquium could be organized to review legal issues and challenges related to digital payments and to take stock of existing international and regional instruments and efforts by other organizations, and that the secretariat should report back to the Commission on the desirability and feasibility of developing harmonized standards. In that context, the need was underlined to carefully consider any intersection with existing regulatory frameworks so as to ensure that the exploratory work would clearly define the scope and the legal issues that were to be addressed and that that work would fall within the mandate of the Commission.

## D. Working methods of UNCITRAL

### 1. Streamlining General Assembly resolutions on UNCITRAL annual reports

271. The Commission recalled that, at its fifty-seventh session, it had requested the secretariat to continue to facilitate an open and flexible intersessional consultative process led in Vienna among States Members of the United Nations, which had been initiated in 2023 and had been expanded to involve UNCITRAL focal points of member and observer States.[67]

272. The Commission noted that, since its fifty-seventh session, seven informal consultations had been convened, on 10 September 2024, 7 October 2024, 17 January 2025, 2 June 2025, and 14 and 15 July 2025, which had been coordinated by Panama.

273. The Commission considered a proposal submitted to the secretariat by the Government of Panama, which contained proposed changes to the text of General Assembly resolution 79/117 as the outcome of the intersessional consultative process. In that proposal, it was suggested that the Commission: (a) take note of the proposed changes; (b) request the secretariat to communicate those changes to States Members of the United Nations through their Permanent Missions based in Vienna; and (c) recommend that the proposed changes be taken into account when the General Assembly considered the UNCITRAL omnibus resolution in the fall of 2025.

274. Broad support was expressed for the intersessional process coordinated by Panama. It was mentioned that the proposed changes should not be considered to reflect consensus and that it would be prudent not to have the Commission make a recommendation as proposed in point (c) of the previous paragraph. In that context, Austria expressed its willingness, as the facilitator of UNCITRAL omnibus resolutions, to take into account the outcome of the intersessional consultative process in preparing the draft omnibus resolution.

275. After discussion, the Commission noted with appreciation the progress achieved throughout the entire intersessional consultative process. It also noted that, as a preliminary outcome of that process, the operative paragraphs of General Assembly resolution 79/117, adopted on 4 December 2024, had been reorganized and placed under thematic headings. The Commission requested that the outcome of that process be communicated by the secretariat to States Members of the United Nations through their Permanent Missions based in Vienna. Lastly, the Commission expressed its appreciation to Panama for coordinating the intersessional consultative process and expressed its satisfaction with the service provided by the secretariat.

---

[67] Ibid., *Seventy-ninth Session, Supplement No. 17* (A/79/17), para. 305.

### 2. Possible future cost-saving and efficiency-enhancing measures

276. The Commission was informed of measures under consideration within the United Nations at large to enhance efficiency and of the potential impact of the proposed budget reductions on the secretariat.

277. The Commission noted the possible cost-saving measures proposed by the Governments of Germany, Israel and Switzerland as well as those suggested by the delegations of France and Canada during the session with regard to the discontinuation of the practice of rotating meeting venues between New York and Vienna and the holding of virtual/hybrid meetings, respectively.

278. The Commission requested the secretariat to compile the proposed measures and to analyse the related budget savings and their implications for the functioning of the Commission, the working groups and the secretariat. It was stressed that the inclusive nature of the work of the Commission should be preserved and that the measures should not result in a reduction in the Commission's activities or output.

279. The Commission agreed to engage in consultations regarding the various proposals to enhance the efficiency of the Commission during the intersessional period and asked the secretariat to facilitate those consultations. The secretariat was also requested to summarize the outcomes of consultations and to present the summary, along with an overall budget analysis, to the Commission at its next session so that the Commission could make an informed decision.

280. In addition, the Commission welcomed the proposal for the delegate of Mexico to take up the role of coordinating the consultative process, which was aimed at revisiting the working methods of UNCITRAL so as to increase efficiency, at achieving cost savings and at enabling the Commission and the secretariat to adapt to new realities, and which would involve UNCITRAL focal points of member and observer States not only from Vienna-based permanent missions but also from capitals.

### 3. Livestreaming of sessions

281. The Commission was apprised of the financial resources needed to livestream Commission and working group sessions (totalling up to 16 weeks per year, A/CN.9/1210, paras. 41–43). Noting that livestreaming the sessions would increase the inclusiveness of the process and could result in cost savings for delegates, the Commission agreed to recommend to the General Assembly that it grant the Commission the necessary resources to allow the livestreaming of Commission and working group sessions.

### 4. Project proposal template for future work

282. The Commission heard a suggestion for a project proposal template to be used when formulating proposals for future work by the Commission. It was noted that the proposed template should be in line with the decisions by the Commission on criteria for assessing whether a topic should be referred to a working group.[68]

283. The Commission recommended that the proposed template be communicated to member States wishing to make proposals for future work. In that regard, it was suggested that States should continue to have the flexibility to submit proposals in different forms and that the absence of information recommended in the template should not be a basis for rejecting a proposal, as the information might not be known to the proposing State. The secretariat was asked to make the template and related guidance available on the website of the Commission.

[68] Ibid., *Sixty-eighth Session, Supplement No. 17* (A/68/17), paras. 303 and 304.

## E. Resources to implement the work programme with respect to investor-State dispute settlement reform

284. The Commission considered the resource requirements to finalize the investor-State dispute settlement reform project on the basis of document A/CN.9/1217, focusing its deliberations on whether it would recommend to the General Assembly that additional conference time and supporting resources be allocated to the secretariat for an extended period of two years (2026–2027).

285. The Commission noted that Working Group III had, at its fiftieth session, considered the possible implications of the expiry of the additional resources and how the Working Group could continue its work on the basis of the workplan reproduced in A/CN.9/1217.[69]

286. Broad support was expressed for recommending the allocation of additional resources to maintain the momentum of the investor-State dispute settlement reform project, although some concerns were raised, as set forth below. The proposed workplan was generally viewed as balanced, as it envisaged the completion of the investor-State dispute settlement reform project in a reasonable time period while taking into account different interests.

287. The importance and urgency of investor-State dispute settlement reform, particularly for developing countries, was emphasized. The reform elements that were crucial to those countries were also highlighted. The continuation of the work was seen as essential for achieving meaningful reform outcomes, and the view was expressed that by approving the additional resources, the Commission would demonstrate its commitment to supporting the important process.

288. The need to ensure inclusiveness and transparency was stressed. In that context, it was noted that livestreaming working group sessions would increase the inclusiveness of the process and could result in cost savings for delegates. It was recalled that the Commission had agreed to recommend to the General Assembly that it grant the Commission the necessary resources to allow the livestreaming of Commission and working group sessions (see para. 281 above).

289. It was further noted that the services provided by the secretariat to the investor-State dispute settlement reform project were well balanced with those provided to other working groups and the overall work programme of the Commission, and that the resources being sought would make it possible to preserve the fair balance of work among the different workstreams of the Commission.

290. However, it was noted that for certain delegations, limited human resources and competing commitments often hindered their full participation in the meetings of Working Group III. Concerns were also raised about the increasing number of informal processes, including intersessional meetings, that were being held in parallel to formal sessions. It was stated that the necessity and frequency of such informal meetings should be carefully considered. In that context, it was stressed that measures should be taken to ensure the broad participation of delegates in such processes, including through hybrid meetings and the provision of travel support for delegates from developing countries.

291. A view was expressed that it would not be appropriate for the Commission to recommend the extension of additional resources. It was explained that the allocation of additional resources by the General Assembly in 2021 was for a single period of four years, and that an extension would not be justified. Furthermore, the lack of consensus on certain elements of investor-State dispute settlement reform could not be resolved by increasing the frequency and number of meetings. Moreover, such a request would be inappropriate in light of the current financial situation at the United

[69] A/CN.9/1195, paras. 137 and 138. The Working Group had considered the implications on the basis of the information in chapter III of document A/CN.9/WG.III/WP.248.

Nations; the Working Group should instead focus on better identifying its priorities and seek to achieve those priorities within existing resources.

292. Noting those concerns, the Commission reiterated that progress should continue to be made in a constructive manner and in accordance with the updated workplan.[70] While emphasizing the need to take a flexible approach in carrying out the work and to adapt the workplan, which was notional, to the current needs of the Working Group, the Commission requested the Working Group to continue its work in an effective manner and encouraged it to present concrete substantive reform elements at its next session.

293. After discussion and on the basis of strong support, the Commission decided to recommend to the General Assembly that additional conference time and supporting resources be allocated to the secretariat for a period of two more years, from 2026 to 2027, as outlined in document A/CN.9/1217. Nonetheless, one delegation reiterated the reservation that it had expressed concerning that decision (see para. 291 above).

# XVII. Coordination and cooperation

## A. General

294. The Commission had before it a note by the Secretariat providing information on the activities of international organizations in the field of international trade law in which the secretariat had participated during the 2024 calendar year (A/CN.9/1211). The Commission thanked the secretariat for closely following the work of other organizations and for coordinating with them the implementation of their respective work programmes, in particular HCCH and UNIDROIT. It was stressed that such efforts assisted the Commission in implementing its mandate to coordinate the work of organizations active in the field of international trade law and to encourage cooperation among them.[71]

295. The Commission recalled the joint work carried out on the UNCITRAL-UNIDROIT Model Law on Warehouse Receipts (2024) and the UNCITRAL-UNIDROIT study on the legal nature of verified carbon credits issued by independent carbon standard setters.[72] The Commission noted with appreciation the cooperation between its secretariat and the HCCH and UNIDROIT secretariats with respect to the development of the UNCITRAL Toolkit and Background Notes on Asset Tracing and Recovery in Insolvency Proceedings, which had been adopted at the current session and whose preface acknowledged the valuable contributions of the HCCH Permanent Bureau and the UNIDROIT secretariat and Working Group on Best Practices for Effective Enforcement. The Commission also noted with appreciation inputs by the secretariat and its participation in deliberations on the following projects: (a) projects being developed by HCCH, including the Digital Economy Project, under which developments regarding digital platforms, artificial intelligence and automated contracting, and immersive technologies were being monitored, and the Digital Tokens Project, under which, among other things, the Model Law on Electronic Transferable Records had been identified as a use case and which would support the implementation of the Model Law; and (b) projects being developed by UNIDROIT, including with the working groups on bank insolvency, on best practices for effective enforcement, on factoring, on international investment contracts and on the legal nature of verified carbon credits.

296. The Commission was also informed that the tripartite coordination meeting of the UNCITRAL, UNIDROIT and HCCH secretariats had been held in June 2025, at which a revised draft of the Coordination Guidelines for the Secretariats of HCCH, UNCITRAL and UNIDROIT had been discussed. The Commission had before it the

[70] See A/CN.9/WG.III/WP.248, pp. 11 and 12.

[71] General Assembly resolution 2205 (XXI), sect. II, para. 8(a).

[72] A/CN.9/1191/Rev.1.

finalized Coordination Guidelines, which were intended to facilitate and strengthen cooperation and coordination between the three secretariats. The Commission welcomed the commitment of the secretariats to continue working closely together to achieve greater coordination of their respective work programmes, agendas, meeting dates and timelines, including through the implementation of the Coordination Guidelines, in order to ensure the efficient use of resources and to avoid overlap and fragmentation. In view of the overlapping mandates and projects of the three organizations, the view was expressed that their States members should continue to be attentive to their work programmes, in order to help each organization make the best use of scarce resources.

297. It was stated that the UNCITRAL secretariat played a positive and productive role in coordinating activities, both within and outside the United Nations system. It was also stated that, as the Asia-Pacific region accounted for significant economic growth, the UNCITRAL secretariat should explore ways to enhance cooperation with organizations from that region. More generally, the Commission expressed its satisfaction with the secretariat's coordination activities, both at the general level and in relation to specific topics forming part of the Commission's work programme, including with the following organizations and forums: (a) within the United Nations system: the Economic and Social Commission for Asia and the Pacific, the Economic and Social Commission for Western Asia, the Office for Digital and Emerging Technologies, the Statistics Division, UNCTAD, the United Nations Centre for Facilitation of Procedures and Practices for Administration, Commerce and Transport and the World Bank Group; and (b) outside the United Nations system: AALCO, the Comité Maritime International, the Commonwealth, the Eurasian Economic Commission, HCCH, the Intergovernmental Organisation for International Carriage by Rail, the Joint Network for Coordinating and Supporting Secured Transactions Reforms, OECD, the Organisation for Co-operation between Railways, PCA, UNIDROIT and WTO.

298. The Commission noted with interest both the *Governing AI for Humanity: Final Report* published by the Secretary-General's High-level Advisory Body on Artificial Intelligence, which recommended the creation of a global artificial intelligence data framework developed through a process initiated by a relevant agency, such as UNCITRAL, and informed by the work of other international organizations, and the steps taken by the secretariat to formalize its participation in the multi-stakeholder working group on data governance at all levels envisaged in the Global Digital Compact. The Commission also noted the reference to the work of UNCITRAL in the Sevilla Commitment, in which support was expressed for efforts to reform the mechanisms for investor-State dispute settlement in trade and investment agreements, including through a multilateral approach towards the establishment of the Advisory Centre on International Investment Dispute Resolution, and building on the ongoing work of UNCITRAL.[73]

299. The Commission reiterated the importance of coordinating the activities of organizations active in the field of international trade law, which was a core element of the mandate that UNCITRAL had received from the General Assembly, as a means of avoiding duplication of efforts and promoting efficiency, consistency and coherence in the harmonization, unification and modernization of international trade law.

## B. Reports of other international organizations

300. The Commission took note of the statements made on behalf of international organizations, including intergovernmental and non-governmental organizations, invited to the session, which focused on activities of relevance to UNCITRAL.

[73] A/CONF.227/2025/L.1, annex, para. 43 (l).

### 1. Asian-African Legal Consultative Organization

301. The Commission heard a statement by AALCO noting in particular that:

(a) AALCO regularly discussed the work of UNCITRAL at its annual sessions and strongly promoted UNCITRAL texts and guidance;

(b) AALCO had established six regional arbitration centres that utilized institutional rules largely based on the UNCITRAL Arbitration Rules;

(c) States members of AALCO were actively involved in the investor-State dispute settlement reform work being carried out in Working Group III and had endorsed that work at the Organization's annual meeting, held in Bangkok from 9 to 13 September 2024, in particular the adoption in principle of the Statute of the Advisory Centre on International Investment Dispute Resolution.

### 2. Commonwealth secretariat

302. The representative of the Commonwealth secretariat expressed appreciation for the provision by UNCITRAL of crucial support on legal reform and digitalization efforts to States members of the Commonwealth, particularly developing and small island States, and noted:

(a) The development of the Commonwealth Model Law on Digital Trade, which had recently been finalized and built on several UNCITRAL e-commerce texts, including the Model Law on Electronic Transferable Records, the Model Law on the Use and Cross-border Recognition of Identity Management and Trust Services and the Model Law on Automated Contracting;

(b) The intention to deepen coordination with UNCITRAL, including to continue supporting the development of cross-border paperless trade.

### 3. Hague Conference on Private International Law

303. The Secretary-General of HCCH reported on areas of continued cooperation between HCCH and UNCITRAL, noting, in particular:

(a) The close relationship that HCCH had with UNCITRAL and UNIDROIT, and that the HCCH Permanent Bureau had made a point of including relevant UNCITRAL and UNIDROIT colleagues in its activities and of promoting UNCITRAL and UNIDROIT instruments in its work;

(b) Apart from the work at HCCH on international family and child protection law, the respective mandates and work programmes had regularly given rise to close cooperation and the need for transparent coordination;

(c) The finalization of the Coordination Guidelines, the development of which had been proposed by the HCCH Permanent Bureau in April 2023.

### 4. International Institute for the Unification of Private Law

304. The Secretary-General of UNIDROIT reported on developments concerning several UNIDROIT activities, including:

(a) Two recent examples of cooperation between UNIDROIT and UNCITRAL, in particular the Model Law on Warehouse Receipts, and the UNCITRAL-UNIDROIT study on the legal nature of verified carbon credits issued by independent carbon standard setters, as well as the finalization of the Coordination Guidelines, which would facilitate coordination going forward;

(b) The upcoming celebration planned by UNIDROIT to mark its 100th anniversary, at which representatives of UNCITRAL and HCCH would have lead roles;

(c) The recent adoption of the UNIDROIT Legislative Guide on Bank Liquidation and of the Guide to Enactment of the UNIDROIT Model Law on Factoring, the endorsement of the draft instrument on best practices for effective enforcement, and the ongoing development of an instrument on investment contracts, all of which had benefited from input by the UNCITRAL secretariat.

### 5. International Organisation of La Francophonie

305. The Commission heard a statement by the International Organisation of La Francophonie welcoming the excellent collaboration between the Organisation and UNCITRAL since 2019 to mobilize and strengthen the participation of French-speaking countries, particularly African ones, in the discussions of UNCITRAL Working Group III on investor-State dispute settlement reform, given the significant challenges facing some of them in terms of sustainable economic development. The collaboration had made it possible to organize workshops and remote meetings on various reform elements important to such countries.

### 6. Permanent Court of Arbitration

306. The representative of PCA made a statement providing an overview of the experience of PCA in 2024 with UNCITRAL texts and addressing its cooperation with Working Groups II and III. The Commission was informed of the experience of PCA in providing registry support for international arbitration conducted under the UNCITRAL Arbitration Rules (including the 1976, 2010, 2013 and 2021 versions) and the role of the Secretary-General of PCA as designating authority or appointing authority under those Rules and, in the 2010 and subsequent versions, in the review of arbitrator fees. The Commission noted with satisfaction the contributions made by PCA to the work of Working Groups II and III, as well as its participation in the operationalization of the Advisory Centre on International Investment Dispute Resolution.

### 7. Center for International Legal Studies

307. The representative of the Center for International Legal Studies expressed appreciation for the secretariat's coordination efforts, which were necessary to avoid overlap and fragmentation, and suggested that the publication entitled "UNCITRAL, Hague Conference and UNIDROIT Texts on Security Interests" be updated.

### 8. China Society of Private International Law

308. The representative of the China Society of Private International Law expressed appreciation for the coordination efforts, noting that UNCITRAL, UNIDROIT and HCCH had shaped the landscape of international trade law, private law and private international law, respectively. As there had been instances of overlap in their work, the representative suggested that consideration be given to coordinating work on a thematic basis.

### 9. International Chamber of Commerce

309. The representative of ICC, who also spoke on behalf of the ICC Digital Standards Initiative and the ICC Banking Commission, expressed appreciation for the long-standing cooperation between ICC and UNCITRAL and highlighted the following two examples of such cooperation:

(a) The engagement of the ICC Digital Standards Initiative with Working Group IV, that engagement having been instrumental in promoting a globally interoperable digital trade ecosystem underpinned by legal certainty. As jurisdictions moved towards implementing the Model Law on Electronic Transferable Records, the Digital Standards Initiative remained committed to supporting the legal reform process and technical standardization necessary to ensure real-world usability;

(b) The engagement of the ICC Banking Commission with Working Group VI, particularly on the recently approved draft convention on negotiable cargo documents, which would provide legal certainty for trade digitalization and the negotiability of transport documents.

### C. International governmental and non-governmental organizations invited to sessions of UNCITRAL and its working groups

310. The Commission had before it a note by the Secretariat providing information about intergovernmental and non-governmental organizations invited to attend sessions of UNCITRAL and its working groups (A/CN.9/1212). The note had been prepared pursuant to the Commission's request, at its fiftieth session, that such information be submitted in writing for future sessions.[74] The Commission noted the non-governmental organizations newly admitted since its previous session, as well as those whose applications had been declined. It also noted updates concerning the separate list of additional non-governmental organizations invited exclusively to sessions of Working Group III while it continued its work on investor-State dispute settlement reform.

## XVIII. Non-legislative activities

### A. Commission actions in relation to the reports of non-legislative activities held in 2024

311. For its consideration of the sub-item on Commission actions on the reports of non-legislative activities held in 2024, the Commission had before it notes by the Secretariat (A/CN.9/1209 and A/CN.9/1209/Add.1–9). The Commission expressed appreciation to its secretariat for the non-legislative activities carried out in 2024 and noted the resource-intensive nature of those activities. It further noted that the austerity measures imposed by the United Nations, in particular a hiring freeze, would make it impossible to sustain those activities in 2025 and subsequent years unless the shortage of human resources was addressed through extrabudgetary resources (e.g. the engagement of individual contractors, consultants, junior professional officers, gratis personnel (for example, personnel seconded from Governments on non-reimbursable loans) or other temporary assistance). The Commission was informed that the operationalization of the Advisory Centre on International Investment Dispute Resolution and other non-legislative activities emanating from the work of Working Group III on investor-State dispute settlement reform required additional human and financial resources to avoid reallocation of the already limited resources available in the UNCITRAL secretariat for non-legislative activities to the intensive non-legislative work related to investor-State dispute settlement reform, which was expected to increase in volume and scope in the coming years. In that regard, the Commission expressed appreciation to Switzerland for the announced plan to contribute to the trust fund for UNCITRAL symposiums, in support of the secretariat's technical assistance activities in the area of investor-State dispute settlement reform.

312. With regard to document A/CN.9/1209/Add.1, which listed selected technical assistance activities carried out by the UNCITRAL secretariat in 2024,[75] the Commission noted the technical cooperation and assistance activities that had been conducted in 2024, including: (a) UNCITRAL Days in four regions (Africa, the Arab States, Asia and the Pacific, and Latin America and the Caribbean); (b) the UNCITRAL Academy 2024, jointly organized by the secretariat and the Singapore Ministry of Law under the memorandum of understanding with Singapore; (c) the international symposiums and seminars in China under the memorandum of understanding with China; (d) a high-level discussion on the theme "Emerging trends in digital trade law" and other activities under the memorandum of understanding

[74] *Official Records of the General Assembly, Seventy-second Session, Supplement No. 17* (A/72/17), para. 364.

[75] Additional activities were brought to the attention of the Commission through an informal document made available on the web page of its current session (https://uncitral.un.org/en/commission).

with Saudi Arabia; (e) UNCITRAL-related events within the framework of the Asia-Pacific Economic Cooperation Forum held in Peru in 2024, the Economic and Social Commission for Asia and the Pacific paperless trade facilitation programme, the UNCTAD "eTrade for all" initiative and the Central Asia Regional Economic Cooperation Programme and International Trade Centre digital trade and related activities in Central Asia; (f) the preparation in English and Spanish of a curriculum for training judges on the basis of the UNCITRAL cross-border insolvency framework, and the launch of that training in Panama in Spanish in November 2024; (g) the Fourteenth Multinational Judicial Colloquium on Insolvency, organized with INSOL International and the World Bank Group; (h) a conference on UNCITRAL insolvency law in the Balkan region, organized with the European Bank for Reconstruction and Development; (i) activities organized within the framework of the Joint Network for Coordinating and Supporting Secured Transactions Reform; and (j) "Transparency@10" events organized worldwide. It expressed appreciation for the efforts of the UNCITRAL secretariat to take a holistic and interdisciplinary approach to the promotion, through those activities, of the adoption and use of UNCITRAL texts and their uniform application and interpretation. It also expressed appreciation to all concerned for the support provided to the secretariat with the implementation of those activities.

313. The Commission noted with interest examples of national commercial law reform following the delivery by the UNCITRAL secretariat of technical assistance activities in the States concerned. The view was expressed that the value of adopting UNCITRAL texts increased with their uptake by the intended stakeholders, and that such uptake was facilitated by the secretariat's technical assistance activities. The secretariat was commended for its efforts and was requested to expand those activities and to broaden the outreach of UNCITRAL Days. The relevance of the activities to addressing national development goals and challenges was highlighted. Some delegations offered opportunities for cooperation with the UNCITRAL secretariat in those activities, including by supporting the organization of UNCITRAL Days through domestic programmes for academic institutions. The Commission was also informed of a relevant development in the World Bank Group, namely, the establishment of the Law Advisory and Knowledge Unit under the Legal Vice Presidency.

314. With regard to document A/CN.9/1209/Add.2, on selected activities of the UNCITRAL Regional Centre for Asia and the Pacific in 2024, including its flagship events, the 2024 UNCITRAL Asia-Pacific Days and support provided to the UNCITRAL secretariat based in Vienna,[76] the Commission noted those activities, including related statistics, and the current resources and funding situation of the Regional Centre. It noted with appreciation, in particular, the growing popularity and positive outcomes of the Regional Centre's annual flagship events (the special session on alternative dispute resolution hosted by the Ministry of Justice of the Republic of Korea and UNCITRAL, and the Asia-Pacific Alternative Dispute Resolution Conference) and the increased areas of law covered by the Regional Centre's activities. It expressed appreciation to the Government of the Republic of Korea and the government of Hong Kong, China, for their continued contributions to the operation of the Regional Centre and to all concerned for providing support to the Regional Centre to facilitate the implementation of its mandate. It reiterated its appeal to relevant stakeholders for the provision of additional resources and other support to the Regional Centre and requested States Members of the United Nations to assist the secretariat in identifying sources of funding within their Governments to support the Regional Centre's activities. In that regard, the Commission welcomed the announcement by Japan of its initial financial contribution of $196,410 to the trust fund for UNCITRAL symposiums, made under its memorandum of understanding concluded with the United Nations in January 2025, to support the activities of the Regional Centre. The Commission noted with appreciation that country's plans to

[76] Ibid.

contribute a legal expert to the Regional Centre under a separate memorandum of understanding to be concluded with the United Nations in the near future.

315. With regard to document A/CN.9/1209/Add.3, on ways and means of ensuring a uniform interpretation and application of international conventions and uniform laws in the field of the law of international trade, the Commission:

(a) Noted developments and statistics with respect to the CLOUT system, including an increased number of abstracts from China and from jurisdictions not previously represented in the CLOUT collection, and on UNCITRAL texts not previously covered. It requested those States that had not yet designated a national correspondent or a member of the steering committee to do so at the earliest opportunity and asked all States that had designated national correspondents to facilitate their role and encourage the regular submission by them of high-quality CLOUT abstracts to the secretariat, which would serve as the basis for the preparation of UNCITRAL digests of case law;

(b) Noted progress made in the preparation of digests of case law on UNCITRAL texts. Recalling the plans of the secretariat to prepare an analytical compilation of case law on the Convention on the Limitation Period in the International Sale of Goods as amended by the Protocol of 11 April 1980, which could be annexed to a new edition of the *UNCITRAL Digest of Case Law on the United Nations Convention on Contracts for the International Sale of Goods*, the Commission called on all concerned to assist the secretariat with the collection of relevant case law from more jurisdictions;

(c) Noted that the CLOUT database and the transparency repository could not be maintained by the United Nations Information Technology Service in their current outdated format and urgently required modernization. The Commission appealed to all interested States, organizations, institutions and individuals to consider making contributions to the trust fund for UNCITRAL symposiums earmarked for the purpose of upgrading those databases;

(d) Noted progress made by the UNCITRAL secretariat in its consultations with relevant database and search engine platforms with a view to increasing the dissemination of CLOUT materials, subject to ensuring the multilingual availability of abstracts, free access to them and the recognition and protection of United Nations copyright, as set out in the report of the Commission on its fifty-seventh session.[77]

316. With reference to document A/CN.9/1209/Add.4, on the operation of the transparency repository under article 8 of the UNCITRAL Rules on Transparency in Treaty-based Investor-State Arbitration,[78] the Commission expressed appreciation for the increased promotional (awareness-raising and capacity-building) activities related to the transparency repository and the UNCITRAL transparency standards that had been carried out in 2024 on the occasion of the tenth anniversary of those standards, in particular during the UNCITRAL Days held in Asia and the Pacific and Latin America and the Caribbean in 2024, as also highlighted in paragraph 312 (j) above. It noted positive developments in the uptake of those standards. The Commission also expressed appreciation to the European Union and the Federal Ministry for Economic Cooperation and Development of Germany for providing funding that had made it possible for the Secretary-General to continue to operate, through the secretariat of the Commission, the transparency repository until the end of 2027.

317. With regard to document A/CN.9/1209/Add.5, the Commission noted developments and statistics with respect to the UNCITRAL website, including a notable increase in the number of visitors to its Chinese and English language web pages, and expressed appreciation for the continued efforts of the secretariat to maintain the UNCITRAL website in the six official languages of the United Nations.

[77] *Official Records of the General Assembly, Seventy-ninth Session, Supplement No. 17* (A/79/17), para. 334.

[78] Ibid., *Sixty-eighth Session, Supplement No. 17* (A/68/17), annex I.

Expressing its appreciation to China, Saudi Arabia, the International Training Centre of the International Labour Organization and the European Bank for Reconstruction and Development for their support with the development of the UNCITRAL e-learning programme, the Commission noted with appreciation the addition of an insolvency course to that programme[79] and the translation of some previous courses into Arabic, Chinese and Russian on the website. The Commission reiterated the need for all courses to be translated into the six official languages of the United Nations and appealed for voluntary contributions to the trust fund for UNCITRAL symposiums for that purpose. Lastly, the Commission noted the results of the surveys carried out in 2024 (A/CN.9/1209/Add.5, para. 7) in response to its request at the fifty-seventh session for the secretariat to take innovative approaches to increasing the Commission's presence on various social media platforms in order to raise awareness of the work of UNCITRAL, in particular among younger generations.[80] Those survey results demonstrated that: (a) for the delivery of UNCITRAL-related content, platforms for professionals were more suitable than platforms with a broader appeal and with a visual focus; and (b) the time and resources required to maintain a presence and the engagement of viewers on those latter platforms might not be commensurate with the very small number of followers engaged with the topic of international trade law on those platforms. The Commission expressed appreciation to the secretariat for the conduct of those surveys and their informative results and encouraged it to continue exploring and expanding the presence of UNCITRAL on social media channels, as appropriate and resources permitting, including by involving interns.

318. With regard to document A/CN.9/1209/Add.6, on the UNCITRAL Law Library, publications, press releases and other outreach activities (e.g. press releases and information lectures), the Commission noted the relevant statistics and the commencement by the secretariat of work on the update of the publication *A Guide to UNCITRAL: Basic facts about the United Nations Commission on International Trade Law* for the sixtieth anniversary of the establishment of UNCITRAL on 17 December 1966, the Commission having been informed of those plans at its fifty-seventh session.[81] It also noted other developments related to publications, including contributions by the secretariat to periodicals, reports and other writings relevant to the work of UNCITRAL. It took note of the bibliography of recent writings related to the work of UNCITRAL (A/CN.9/1206) and noted that the consolidated bibliography contained 12,702 entries. The Commission appealed to publishers, especially those representing or affiliated with organizations invited to UNCITRAL sessions, to donate their books, periodicals and other materials related to the work of UNCITRAL or international commercial law to the UNCITRAL Law Library or, where donation was not possible, to grant a discounted rate for such materials. The Commission expressed its appreciation to those publishers that had already done so. It also reiterated its request to States to advise the secretariat when enacting legislation implementing an UNCITRAL model law or other relevant texts..

319. With reference to document A/CN.9/1209/Add.7, the Commission noted the information about internships in the UNCITRAL secretariat (both in Vienna and at the UNCITRAL Regional Centre for Asia and the Pacific), in particular mixed experiences with remote internships. It noted with concern the slight underrepresentation of candidates for internships in Vienna from African and Latin American States, as well as candidates with proficient Arabic and Russian language skills. The Commission encouraged efforts by all concerned to ensure equitable representation, inclusivity, multilingualism and other objectives of the United Nations internship programme in the internship programme of the secretariat, and requested States and observer organizations to bring internship opportunities in the UNCITRAL secretariat to the attention of interested persons and to consider granting scholarships

[79] https://uncitral.un.org/en/onlinecourses.

[80] *Official Records of the General Assembly, Seventy-ninth Session, Supplement No. 17* (A/79/17), para. 341.

[81] Ibid., para. 344.

for the purpose of attracting the most qualified candidates, particularly from underrepresented regions and States. The Commission noted with satisfaction that moot competitions supported by the secretariat remained attractive to students, practitioners and organizing institutions, as one of the most effective means of increasing interest and knowledge in international commercial law among future lawyers.

320. The Commission noted the upcoming activities listed in document A/CN.9/1209/Add.8, stressing their importance and encouraging all concerned to contribute to them, including by disseminating information about them to relevant stakeholders. The Commission heard updates regarding those events, in particular that:

(a) The workshop on the use of international instruments to legally enable end-to-end digitalization of trade would be held by UNCITRAL and the Asia-Pacific Economic Cooperation Forum in person in Incheon, Republic of Korea, on 9 August 2025;

(b) The fourteenth Asia-Pacific Alternative Dispute Resolution Conference would be held in Seoul on 29 October 2025, with the special session on alternative dispute resolution hosted by the Ministry of Justice of the Republic of Korea and UNCITRAL held in a hybrid format on either 28 or 30 October 2025;

(c) Invitations to nominate judges to participate in the third session of the UNCITRAL-World Bank Group Judicial Capacity-Building Initiative on International Best Practices in the Area of Insolvency Law, focusing on safeguards against the improper use of insolvency proceedings, had been circulated to States with the updated information about the session, and efforts were being made by the secretariat to identify partners that could provide interpretation during the session, which the Commission welcomed;

(d) The Japan International Arbitration Week would be held in Tokyo from 25 to 29 November 2025, with the Tokyo Forum on Dispute Resolution being held on 26 November 2025;

(e) The sixth UNCITRAL Asia Pacific Judicial Summit would be held in Hong Kong, China, on 1 and 2 December 2025, immediately after the joint network meeting to be hosted by the UNCITRAL secretariat in Hong Kong, China, on 27 and 28 November 2025.

321. With regard to resources and funding for its non-legislative activities, as set out in document A/CN.9/1209/Add.9, the Commission expressed appreciation for the contributions made to the trust fund for UNCITRAL symposiums and the trust fund established to provide travel assistance to developing countries that are members of UNCITRAL. It renewed its appeal to Governments, the relevant bodies of the United Nations system, organizations, institutions and individuals to make voluntary contributions to those trust funds, to finance special projects and to otherwise assist the secretariat in carrying out non-legislative activities, in light of the steadily increasing demand for them and the impact that focused and well-coordinated activities could have on advancing the mandate of UNCITRAL. With respect to the announced contribution by Switzerland (see para. 311 above), the Commission noted that the contribution had been made possible through the cooperation of relevant line ministries in Switzerland, and that that positive experience could inform approaches to encouraging contributions to the UNCITRAL trust funds in other States.

322. In addition to the matters noted in the preceding paragraphs, the Commission was informed that resources were needed to maintain and upgrade other supporting tools and functions within the UNCITRAL secretariat, such as a SharePoint-based online database for storing records of the secretariat's legislative and non-legislative activities. The Commission noted with appreciation that contributions by China and Saudi Arabia to the trust fund for UNCITRAL symposiums made the implementation of that database possible, and noted that it would be necessary to enhance the database

with AI-enabled capabilities for planning, monitoring, reporting and evaluation purposes in the context of United Nations budgetary and audit processes and donor reporting.

## B. CLOUT Network meeting

323. The Commission reaffirmed its strong support for the CLOUT system, recognizing it as a key tool for promoting the uniform interpretation and application of UNCITRAL texts. It was noted that, as consistently acknowledged by the General Assembly, CLOUT and the digests of case law – based on CLOUT abstracts – not only enabled the monitoring of the implementation of UNCITRAL texts across jurisdictions, but also played a pivotal role in strengthening the capacity of judges, arbitrators and legal practitioners around the world to interpret and apply those standards effectively.

324. The Commission commended the secretariat for organizing the CLOUT Network meeting. It was generally agreed that the meeting had provided a valuable opportunity to review developments related to CLOUT since the previous CLOUT Network meeting, in October 2024. Those developments included achievements and challenges related to the CLOUT system, the status of relevant publications and the relevance of recently adopted UNCITRAL legislative texts.

325. The Commission expressed its appreciation to CLOUT Network members for sharing their experiences, which underscored the value of peer learning and collaboration in advancing the CLOUT objectives. The Commission also noted with appreciation specific examples of the use of CLOUT materials in the UNCITRAL technical assistance and cooperation programme, including judicial capacity-building activities, as well as in the legislative work of UNCITRAL, particularly in the areas of arbitration and insolvency law.

326. The Commission welcomed the secretariat's observations regarding the preparation of case abstracts, in accordance with the CLOUT user guide, aimed at supporting national correspondents and voluntary contributors in improving the quality of their draft abstracts. A suggestion was made for the secretariat to issue an updated CLOUT user guide, which could be supplemented by detailed tutorials that would reflect the secretariat's experience in reviewing draft abstracts. Another suggestion was to establish a uniform time frame for the submission of abstracts by national correspondents.

327. The Commission noted the modern functionalities of external online platforms that could enhance the usability of CLOUT abstracts and ensure their broader dissemination. At the same time, it recalled the parameters for collaboration with such platforms set out by the Commission at its fifty-seventh session (preservation of the multilingual availability of abstracts and of free access to CLOUT materials, as well as the recognition and protection of United Nations copyright (see para. 315 (d) above)).

328. The Commission commended the CLOUT Network for its ongoing consideration of ways to engage academic and training institutions, alongside online platforms, to support the broader dissemination of CLOUT materials. The sixtieth anniversary of UNCITRAL, in 2026, was generally viewed as a timely opportunity to reinvigorate efforts by all interested stakeholders to enrich CLOUT and to increase its visibility, outreach and value. The Commission welcomed the exchange of ideas in that regard at the CLOUT Network meeting, including: (a) the issuance of certificates for the submission of the sixtieth abstract during the celebration year; (b) opportunities to showcase the best abstracts at celebratory events; (c) discussions of how CLOUT could creatively and innovatively be used to implement the UNCITRAL mandate; and (d) side events for academics to exchange their views about trends in interpretation or specific judgments reflected in CLOUT abstracts.

329. The Commission noted various other suggestions aimed at enhancing the CLOUT system and increasing its visibility. They included:

(a) Prompting States to designate a national correspondent for each UNCITRAL text adopted by a State;

(b) Exploring ways to enhance visibility and recognition in the CLOUT system of UNCITRAL texts applied by judges in the absence of the formal adoption of those texts by the State concerned;

(c) Soliciting contributions to CLOUT through UNCITRAL-supported moot competitions and creating appropriate incentives for potential contributors, such as offering complimentary participation in moot courts to students who submitted high-quality CLOUT abstracts;

(d) Developing promotional materials and modern ways to attract new CLOUT contributors and building their capacity to contribute high-quality CLOUT abstracts, including through UNCITRAL Days;

(e) Building more partnerships with CLOUT-like local initiatives that supported activities, programmes and training for students and young professionals;

(f) Sharing best practices regarding States' institutional arrangements related to CLOUT.

# XIX. Status of conventions, model laws and other legal texts emanating from the work of UNCITRAL, as well as the Convention on the Recognition and Enforcement of Foreign Arbitral Awards

330. The Commission considered the status of the conventions and model laws emanating from its work, as well as the status of the 1958 New York Convention, on the basis of a note by the Secretariat (A/CN.9/1207). The Commission noted with appreciation the information on treaty actions and legislative enactments received since its fifty-seventh session.

331. The Commission was informed that El Salvador would deposit its instrument of accession to the Electronic Communications Convention (2005)[82] on 17 July 2025, thus becoming its twentieth State Party. Other delegations shared updates on the respective process for the adoption of UNCITRAL texts.

332. The Commission expressed appreciation to the General Assembly for the support it provided to UNCITRAL in its activities and in performing its distinct role in furthering the dissemination of international commercial law. In particular, the Commission referred to the long-established practice of the General Assembly, upon acting on UNCITRAL texts, to recommend that States give favourable consideration to UNCITRAL texts and to request the Secretary-General to publish UNCITRAL texts, including electronically, in the six official languages of the United Nations and to take other measures to disseminate UNCITRAL texts as broadly as possible to Governments and all other relevant stakeholders. The Commission recalled that in that context, the General Assembly had requested States and other relevant stakeholders, such as organizations active in international commercial law reform, to advise the secretariat when legislation implementing an UNCITRAL model law or other relevant UNCITRAL text had been enacted. The Commission considered it important for States and other stakeholders to do so in order to ensure accurate reporting by the secretariat of the status of UNCITRAL texts.

[82] United Nations, *Treaty Series*, vol. 2898, No. 50525, p. 3.

# XX. Current role of UNCITRAL in promoting the rule of law

## A. Introduction

333. The Commission recalled that the item on the current role of UNCITRAL in promoting the rule of law had been on its agenda since its forty-first session, in 2008,[83] in response to the General Assembly's invitation to the Commission to comment, in its report to the General Assembly, on that matter.[84] The Commission further recalled that, at its forty-first to fifty-seventh sessions, from 2008 to 2024, the Commission, in its annual reports to the General Assembly, had transmitted comments on its role in promoting the rule of law at the national and international levels. At the current session, the Commission had before it a note by the Secretariat on the role of UNCITRAL in promoting the rule of law at the national and international levels (A/CN.9/1223). The Commission noted that the General Assembly, in paragraph 21 of its resolution 79/126, had reiterated its invitation to the Commission to comment on its current role in promoting the rule of law. The Commission further noted that in paragraph 24 of the same resolution, the General Assembly had invited Member States to focus their comments during the upcoming Sixth Committee debate on the subtopic "The rule of law at the national and international levels at the eightieth anniversary of the United Nations".

## B. UNCITRAL comments to the General Assembly

334. In formulating its comments to the General Assembly, the Commission bore in mind the subtopic of the upcoming Sixth Committee debate, "The rule of law at the national and international levels at the eightieth anniversary of the United Nations". The Commission recalled its contributions to the promotion of the rule of law in commercial relations as highlighted in its comments transmitted to the General Assembly in that regard since 2008. In its comments, the Commission noted the relevance to the promotion of the rule of law of the following:

(a) The cooperation and coordination aspect of its mandate,[85] the effective implementation of its technical assistance activities,[86] the building of local capacity in commercial law reforms,[87] and its dissemination activities,[88] which were key to supporting the uniform interpretation and application of UNCITRAL texts;

(b) Its commercial dispute settlement standards, public procurement and other texts and work on investor-State dispute settlement;[89]

(c) For the subtopic on transitional justice in conflict and post conflict situations in 2011, the use and impact of UNCITRAL standards in the reconstruction of post-conflict societies;[90]

---

[83] For the decision of the Commission to include the item on its agenda, see *Official Records of the General Assembly, Sixty-second Session, Supplement No. 17* (A/62/17), part two, paras. 111–113.

[84] General Assembly resolutions 62/70, para. 3; 63/128, para. 7; 64/116, para. 9; 65/32, para. 10; 66/102, para. 12; 67/97, para. 14; 68/116, para. 14; 69/123, para. 17; 70/118, para. 20; 71/148, para. 22; 72/119, para. 25; 73/207, para. 20; 74/191, para. 20; 75/141, para. 20; 76/117, para. 20; 77/110, para. 20; and 78/112, para. 21.

[85] *Official Records of the General Assembly, Sixty-fourth Session, Supplement No. 17* (A/64/17), paras. 414–416.

[86] Ibid., *Sixty-fifth Session, Supplement No. 17* (A/65/17), paras. 315 and 336.

[87] Ibid., *Sixty-seventh Session, Supplement No. 17* (A/67/17), paras. 199–223.

[88] Ibid., *Seventy-second Session, Supplement No. 17* (A/72/17), paras. 435–441.

[89] Ibid., *Sixty-fourth Session, Supplement No. 17* (A/64/17), paras. 417–419; ibid., *Sixty-eighth Session, Supplement No. 17* (A/68/17), paras. 276–290; ibid., *Seventy-third Session, Supplement No. 17* (A/73/17), paras. 232 and 233; ibid., *Seventy-fourth Session, Supplement No. 17* (A/74/17), paras. 299 and 303–308; ibid., *Seventy-sixth Session, Supplement No. 17* (A/76/17), paras. 370–374.

[90] Ibid., *Sixty-sixth Session, Supplement No. 17* (A/66/17), paras. 300 and 316–319.

(d) For the subtopics related to access to justice in 2014, 2016 and 2023, its standards on normative protection, the capacity to seek remedy and effective remedies, the modernization of review procedures and more recent work on the stocktaking of dispute resolution in the digital economy;[91]

(e) Issues arising from multilateral treaty processes at UNCITRAL,[92] and the implementation of multilateral treaties emanating from the work of UNCITRAL;[93]

(f) For the subtopic on preventing and combating corruption in 2020, its work in the area of public procurement and infrastructure development;[94]

(g) For the subtopic on the impacts of the global coronavirus disease (COVID-19) pandemic on the rule of law in 2022, its texts and exploratory work in the areas of electronic commerce, micro-, small and medium-sized enterprises, insolvency, the international sale of goods, public-private partnerships and public procurement, mediation, arbitration and secured transactions;[95]

(h) For the subtopic on full, equal and equitable participation at all levels in the international legal system in 2024, its mandate and working methods.[96]

335. The Commission highlighted how its recent and current work would promote the rule of law and implementation of the Sustainable Development Goals. The Commission heard that over the past eight years, two multilateral treaties had been developed by UNCITRAL and adopted by the General Assembly, namely, the United Nations Convention on International Settlement Agreements Resulting from Mediation[97] (58 signatories, 18 ratifications), and the United Nations Convention on the International Effects of Judicial Sales of Ships[98] (34 signatures, 2 ratifications). The Commission noted that another multilateral treaty, the draft convention on negotiable cargo documents, had been finalized during the current session, reflecting States' commitment to strengthening legal certainty and enforceability in international trade. The Statute of the Advisory Centre on International Investment Dispute Resolution, adopted in principle by the Commission in 2024, was cited as another example of an UNCITRAL text that would help promote the rule of law in the context of international investment disputes.

336. In light of the digital transformation, the Commission noted that the Model Law on Automated Contracting established a legal framework to facilitate the use of automation in the formation and performance of contracts, including through the deployment of artificial intelligence techniques. It was intended to complement and supplement other UNCITRAL texts on electronic commerce and to signal potential intersections with other laws, including an emerging body of law regulating the ethical use and governance of automated systems deploying artificial intelligence techniques. It addressed several fundamental legal issues arising from artificial intelligence and automation in a contractual setting, including: (a) the validity and legal effectiveness of artificial intelligence and automation to form and perform contracts, as well as the use of computer code and dynamic information that powered those transactions; (b) the attribution of "outputs" of artificial intelligence and automated systems; and (c) the legal consequences of "unexpected" outcomes of the use of artificial intelligence and automated systems (as an optional rule). It also recognized the importance of information disclosure in the operation of artificial intelligence and automated systems and acknowledged that such systems could not

[91] Ibid., *Sixty-ninth Session, Supplement No. 17* (A/69/17), paras. 218 and 234–240; ibid., *Seventy-first Session, Supplement No. 17* (A/71/17), paras. 318–342, on related matters; and ibid., *Seventy-eighth Session, Supplement No. 17* (A/78/17), paras. 296–304 on the 2023 subtopic "Using technology to advance access to justice for all".

[92] Ibid., *Seventieth Session, Supplement No. 17* (A/70/17), paras. 302–324.

[93] Ibid., *Seventy-first Session, Supplement No. 17* (A/71/17), para. 306.

[94] Ibid., *Seventy-fifth Session, Supplement No. 17* (A/75/17), paras. 25 and 100–104.

[95] Ibid., *Seventy-seventh Session, Supplement No. 17* (A/77/17), paras. 230–233 and 304–315.

[96] Ibid., *Seventy-ninth Session, Supplement No. 17* (A/79/17), paras. 357–368.

[97] United Nations, *Treaty Series*, vol. 3360, No. 56376.

[98] General Assembly resolution 77/100, annex.

be used simply to avoid or excuse non-compliance with other legal requirements. The Commission noted that the *Governing AI for Humanity: Final Report* published by the Secretary-General's High-level Advisory Body on Artificial Intelligence in September 2024 recommended the creation of a global artificial intelligence data framework and suggested UNCITRAL as a possible forum for such work.[99]

337. The Commission acknowledged that, beyond legislative activities, non-legislative activities of UNCITRAL continued to support the rule of law by aiding States in their commercial law reform efforts, promoting awareness and understanding of international standards and ensuring their implementation and uniform interpretation. Those activities included technical assistance and judicial capacity-building activities, supported by the CLOUT database, digests of case law, online courses, publications and other materials available from the UNCITRAL website.

# XXI. Relevant General Assembly resolutions

338. The Commission recalled that, at its fiftieth session, it had requested the secretariat to replace an oral report to the Commission on relevant General Assembly resolutions with a written report to be issued before the session.[100] Pursuant to that request, the Commission had before it, at its current session, a note by the Secretariat (A/CN.9/1208) summarizing the content of the operative paragraphs of General Assembly resolution 79/117 on the report of the United Nations Commission on International Trade Law on the work of its fifty-seventh session, resolution 79/118 on the Model Law on Warehouse Receipts, and resolution 79/119 on the Model Law on Automated Contracting. The Commission took note of those General Assembly resolutions.

# XXII. Other business

## A. Commemoration of the sixtieth anniversary of the establishment of UNCITRAL

339. The Commission noted that 2026 would mark the sixtieth anniversary of the establishment of UNCITRAL and recognized that milestone as an opportunity to celebrate its significant contributions to the progressive harmonization and modernization of international trade law. The increased participation of developing countries in the work of UNCITRAL in recent years was emphasized. It was noted that the sixtieth anniversary of UNCITRAL could serve as a valuable opportunity to engage member States, past and present, in the commemorative activities and to highlight the impact of UNCITRAL texts within their respective jurisdictions.

340. The Commission observed that the sixtieth anniversary of UNCITRAL would represent a timely occasion to reflect on recent developments in international trade, including the growing importance of digital trade, sustainable development and resilient supply chains. In that context, the Commission reaffirmed the relevance of its mandate to respond to emerging global priorities through the development of legal standards. Emphasis was placed on the importance of ensuring that UNCITRAL would remain fit for purpose in the coming decades and would continue to serve as an inclusive and solution-oriented forum, with even greater participation by developing countries.

341. The Commission was informed that commemorative activities to be hosted by Governments and relevant stakeholders could take various forms (online, in person or hybrid), depending on their needs and preferences. Such activities could include

[99] *Governing AI for Humanity* (United Nations publication, 2024), p. 67.

[100] *Official Records of the General Assembly, Seventy-second Session, Supplement No. 17* (A/72/17), para. 480.

conferences and symposiums, workshops and round-table discussions as well as public awareness campaigns. The Commission called upon Governments and relevant stakeholders to host or support activities to celebrate that significant milestone and further strengthen UNCITRAL and its work.

## B. Evaluation of the role of the UNCITRAL secretariat in facilitating the work of the Commission

342. An online questionnaire on the level of satisfaction of UNCITRAL with the services provided by its secretariat had been sent to States. The Commission was informed that 79 responses had been received and that the level of satisfaction with the services provided by the secretariat remained high. On average, respondents gave a rating of 4.75 out of 5 for "the services and support provided to the Commission" and a rating of 4.65 out of 5 for "the availability of information on the UNCITRAL website".

343. The Commission expressed appreciation to its secretariat for its work.

# XXIII. Date and place of future meetings

## A. Fifty-ninth session of the Commission

344. The Commission approved the holding of its fifty-ninth session in New York, from 22 June to 10 July 2026. Depending on the expected workload of the session, the secretariat was requested to optimize the duration of the session to the extent possible.

## B. Sessions of working groups

345. The Commission considered conference service requirements in light of its work programme, reports of its working groups and a note by the Secretariat (A/CN.9/1217). While proposals were made to adjust the dates of Working Groups III, IV and VI, it was generally felt that the dates as contained in document A/CN.9/1192 provided sufficient time for the working groups and the secretariat to prepare for the sessions. It was recalled that the Commission, at its fifty-seventh session, had emphasized the need to ensure that tentative dates allocated to working groups should remain unchanged to the extent possible,[101] as those dates took into account a number of factors, including the progress of work, the time required for the preparation of working papers and the translation of those documents, and the time required to bring the outcome of the working groups' work to the attention of the Commission.

346. After discussion, the Commission approved the following schedule of working group sessions in the second half of 2025 and in 2026, noting that the second day of the tentative dates for the sixty-ninth session of Working Group IV (21 October 2025) would fall on Diwali, one of the significant holidays of the United Nations. The secretariat was requested to make efforts to avoid the holding of meetings during a holiday of the United Nations.

---

[101] *Official Records of the General Assembly, Seventy-ninth Session, Supplement No. 17* (A/79/17), para. 375.

| | *Second half of 2025 (Vienna)* | *First half of 2026 (New York)* | *Second half of 2026 (Vienna) (to be confirmed by the Commission at its fifty-ninth session, in 2026)* |
|---|---|---|---|
| Working Group I (to be decided) | Forty-second session<br>29 September–3 October 2025 (possible alternative dates: 1 and 2 December 2025 and 19–21 January 2026) | Forty-third session<br>9–13 February 2026 | Forty-fourth session<br>21–25 September 2026 |
| Working Group II (Dispute Settlement) | Eighty-second session<br>13–17 October 2025 | Eighty-third session<br>16–20 February 2026 | Eighty-fourth session<br>28 September–2 October 2026 |
| Working Group III (Investor-State Dispute Settlement Reform) | Fifty-second session<br>22–26 September 2025 | Fifty-third session<br>12–16 January 2026<br>Fifty-fourth session (Vienna)[a]<br>23–27 March 2026 | Fifty-fifth session<br>12–16 October 2026 |
| Working Group IV (Electronic Commerce) | Sixty-ninth session<br>20–24 October 2025 | Seventieth session<br>23–27 March 2026 | Seventy-first session<br>5–9 October 2026 |
| Working Group V (Insolvency Law) | Sixty-seventh session<br>8–12 December 2025 | Sixty-eighth session<br>13–17 April 2026 | Sixty-ninth session<br>16–20 November 2026 |
| Working Group VI (Negotiable Cargo Documents) | Forty-seventh session<br>15–19 December 2025 | Forty-eighth session<br>20–24 April 2026 | Forty-ninth session<br>9–13 November 2026 |

[a] Subject to additional resources being granted by the General Assembly.

347. Recalling its decisions to hold colloquiums on a number of topics, the Commission agreed to hold colloquiums on:

(a) Topics related to insolvency law (see para. 256 above) in conjunction with the Working Group V sessions;

(b) Topics related to dispute resolution in the digital economy (see para. 237 above) in conjunction with the Working Group II sessions;

(c) Topics related to secured transactions, end-to-end trade digitalization, paperless trade, digital platforms and digital payments (either in conjunction or separately), utilizing the conference resources allocated to the forty-second and forty-third sessions of Working Group I, as well as any conference resources of other working groups that may become available.

348. The secretariat was requested to consider holding colloquiums in a hybrid format to allow remote participation, resources permitting.

# Annex I

## Draft convention on negotiable cargo documents

*The States Parties to this Convention,*

*Reaffirming* their belief that international trade on the basis of equality and mutual benefit is a key factor in promoting friendly relations among States,

*Conscious* of the important role played by negotiable transport documents in facilitating trade finance and the sale of goods in transit,

*Convinced* of the desirability of establishing uniform rules for negotiable transport documents covering all modes of transport, including multimodal transport, thereby supporting the growth of door-to-door transportation,

*Acknowledging* that digital transformation in international trade depends on reliable systems and data, which in turn can enhance operational efficiency and support end-to-end digitalization,

*Convinced* that certainty with regard to the legal effect of negotiable cargo documents, as well as the rights and liability of the holder, will encourage the acceptance of such documents by banks, financial institutions and other stakeholders, thereby fostering international trade and contributing to economic growth,

*Convinced also* that a sound legal framework could help reduce the costs of trade along inland routes and will assist both landlocked countries and countries with large mainland territories in integrating more effectively into global supply chains,

*Have agreed* as follows:

## CHAPTER 1. GENERAL PROVISIONS

*Article 1. Scope of application*

1. This Convention applies to the issuance, transfer and legal effects of a negotiable cargo document that contains a conspicuous reference to this Convention in connection with the international transport of goods by one or more than one mode of transport if:

(a) The place of taking in charge of the goods by the transport operator as indicated in the negotiable cargo document is located in a State Party;

(b) The place of delivery of the goods by the transport operator as indicated in the negotiable cargo document is located in a State Party; or

(c) The place of issuance of the negotiable cargo document as indicated in the negotiable cargo document is located in a State Party.

2. This Convention does not affect the application of any international convention or national law relating to the regulation and control of transport operations.

3. Except as otherwise provided for herein, this Convention does not modify the rights and obligations of the transport operator, consignor or consignee or their liability under applicable international conventions or national law governing the transport contract.

*Article 2. Definitions*

For the purposes of this Convention:

1. "Consignor" means a person with whom the transport operator has concluded a transport contract.

2. "Consignee" means a person named in the transport contract as the person entitled to take delivery of the goods.

3. "Electronic record" means information generated, communicated, received or stored by electronic means, including, where appropriate, all information logically associated with, or otherwise linked together so as to become part of, the record, whether generated contemporaneously or not.

4. "Holder" means a person that is in possession of a negotiable cargo document and is identified in it as the consignor, as the person to whose order it is issued or as the person to which the document is duly endorsed, or, if the document is an order document endorsed in blank, is the bearer thereof.

5. "Negotiable cargo document" means a paper document or an electronic record signed and issued by the transport operator that indicates by wording such as "to order" or "negotiable" or an equivalent expression that the goods as specified in the document have been taken in charge by the transport operator and consigned to the order of the holder.

6. "Transport contract" means a contract whereby the transport operator undertakes to perform international transport of goods for reward.

7. "Transport document" means a document that:

(a) Evidences or contains the transport contract; and

(b) Evidences the taking in charge of the goods for transport under the transport contract.

8. "Transport operator" means a person who concludes a transport contract with the consignor and who assumes responsibility for the performance of the contract, irrespective of whether or not that person performs the transport itself.

# CHAPTER 2. ISSUANCE, CONTENT AND LEGAL EFFECT OF NEGOTIABLE CARGO DOCUMENTS

*Article 3. Issuance of a negotiable cargo document*

1. If so agreed between the transport operator and the consignor, the transport operator shall issue a negotiable cargo document, in the medium agreed upon, that contains a conspicuous reference to this Convention.

2. The transport operator and the consignor shall agree on the method of issuing a negotiable cargo document, which may include:

(a) Entering an annotation signed by the transport operator in each original of the transport document; or

(b) Issuing a stand-alone negotiable cargo document where no transport document has been issued or where a transport document has been issued and cancelled.

3. Where the parties have agreed on the method described in paragraph 2 (a) of this article, the annotation shall contain, in a conspicuous manner, the indication set out in article 2, paragraph 5, as well as a statement indicating that the transport document is to serve as a negotiable cargo document from a specified date.

4. The negotiable cargo document shall be issued when the goods are taken in charge by the transport operator. If so agreed between the transport operator and the consignor, where a transport document has been issued, the transport operator may issue the negotiable cargo document at a later stage.

5. The transport operator who issues a negotiable cargo document shall not request the issuance of a negotiable transport document in respect of the goods to which the negotiable cargo document relates.

6. The negotiable cargo document may be made out to order or to the order of a named person. If the negotiable cargo document fails to name the person to whose order it is made out, it shall be deemed to be made out to the order of the consignor.

*Article 4. Contents of the negotiable cargo document*

1. The negotiable cargo document shall indicate:

(a) The name and address of the transport operator;

(b) The name and address of the consignor;

(c) The following particulars as furnished by the consignor: (i) the general nature of the goods; (ii) the leading marks necessary for identification of the goods; (iii) an express statement, if applicable, as to the dangerous character of the goods; (iv) the number of packages or pieces; and (v) the gross weight of the goods or their quantity otherwise expressed;

(d) The apparent order and condition of the goods as taken in charge by the transport operator;

(e) The place and date of taking in charge of the goods by the transport operator;

(f) The place and date of issuance of the negotiable cargo document;

(g) The terms of the transport contract, if issued as a stand-alone negotiable cargo document;

(h) The place of delivery of the goods;

(i) The number of originals of the negotiable cargo document; and

(j) A statement as to whether the freight has been prepaid or an indication as to whether the freight is payable at destination.

2. The negotiable cargo document may further indicate:

(a) The date or the period of delivery of the goods at the place of delivery, if expressly agreed upon between the consignor and the transport operator;

(b) The intended journey route, mode of transport, places of trans-shipment and information enabling tracking of the goods;

(c) The law applicable to the transport contract, in particular any international convention to which the transport contract is subject; and

(d) Any other particulars that the consignor and the transport operator agree to insert in the negotiable cargo document.

*Article 5. Deficiencies in the negotiable cargo document*

1. The absence of one or more of the particulars referred to in article 4, paragraph 1, does not of itself affect the legal effect or validity of the document as a negotiable cargo document provided that the document nevertheless falls within the definition of negotiable cargo document as set out in article 2, paragraph 5.

2. Nothing in paragraph 1 affects the liability of the transport operator under applicable law for any deficiency in the negotiable cargo document.

3. If the negotiable cargo document includes a date but fails to indicate the significance of that date, the date is deemed to be the date of issuance of the negotiable cargo document.

4. If the annotation referred to in article 3, paragraph 3, does not state the date from which the transport document is to serve as a negotiable cargo document, the transport document is deemed to serve that function from the date of its issuance.

5. If the negotiable cargo document does not include the date of taking in charge of the goods by the transport operator, the goods are deemed to have been taken in charge by the transport operator on the date of issuance of the negotiable cargo document.

6. If the negotiable cargo document fails to state the apparent order and condition of the goods at the time the transport operator takes them in charge, it shall be deemed to state that the goods were in apparent good order and condition at the time the transport operator took them in charge.

*Article 6. Evidentiary effect of the negotiable cargo document*

1. The transport operator may qualify any of the information in the negotiable cargo document furnished by the consignor and referred to in article 4, paragraph 1 (c), to indicate that the transport operator does not assume responsibility for the accuracy of such information if it has:

(a) Either actual knowledge or reasonable grounds to believe that any such information is false or misleading; or

(b) No reasonable means of checking such information.

2. Except to the extent that the information furnished by the consignor has been qualified in the manner set out in paragraph 1, the negotiable cargo document shall constitute prima facie evidence of the taking in charge of the goods by the transport operator as stated in the negotiable cargo document.

3. If the negotiable cargo document has been transferred to a third party acting in good faith in reliance on any of the information therein, proof to the contrary by the transport operator in respect of any information in the negotiable cargo document shall not be admissible against that third party, except to the extent that the information furnished by the consignor has been qualified in the manner set out in paragraph 1.

# CHAPTER 3. RIGHTS AND LIABILITY OF THE HOLDER

*Article 7. Rights of the holder of a negotiable cargo document*

1. Upon the issuance of a negotiable cargo document, the rights provided for in the negotiable cargo document can be exercised only by the holder, which shall include the right to demand delivery of the goods at destination.

2. A person other than the consignor who becomes a holder of the negotiable cargo document shall, by virtue of becoming the holder, have acquired the right to bring a claim against the transport operator and, where applicable, the right of disposal under the transport contract, as well as those rights provided for in the law applicable to the transport contract, as if it were a party to that contract.

3. The transport operator may not invoke against a holder that is not the consignor any terms of the transport contract that are inconsistent with the express terms of the negotiable cargo document.

4. The issuance and initial transfer of possession of a negotiable cargo document, as well as any subsequent transfers, to the holder shall have the same effect, for the purpose of acquisition of rights to the goods, as the physical handing over of the goods.

5. In order to exercise its rights, the holder shall present the negotiable cargo document to the transport operator. If the negotiable cargo document states that more than one original has been issued, the holder shall present all originals to exercise the right of disposal.

*Article 8. Missing information, instructions or documents*

If the transport operator needs information, instructions or documents relating to the goods in order to perform its obligations, it shall seek that information or those instructions or documents from the holder of the negotiable cargo document. If the transport operator, after reasonable effort, is unable to obtain that information or those instructions or documents within a reasonable time, it shall proceed in accordance with the transport contract.

*Article 9. Liability of the holder*

1. A holder of the negotiable cargo document that is not the consignor and that does not exercise any right in accordance with article 7 does not assume any liability under the transport contract solely by reason of being a holder of the negotiable cargo document.

2. A holder of the negotiable cargo document that is not the consignor and that exercises a right in accordance with article 7 assumes any liability:

(a) Attributable to the person exercising such a right under the law applicable to the transport contract; or

(b) That arises from the exercise of that right under the transport contract to the extent that such liability is ascertainable from the negotiable cargo document,

as if it were a party to the transport contract.

*Article 10. Delivery of the goods*

1. Delivery of the goods may be demanded from the transport operator only against surrender of the negotiable cargo document by the holder.

2. If more than one original of the negotiable cargo document has been issued, delivery of the goods may be demanded against surrender of one original. If the negotiable cargo document states that more than one original has been issued, the other originals will cease to have any effect or validity after the surrender of one original.

*Article 11. Transfer of rights of the holder*

A holder transfers the rights provided for in the negotiable cargo document to another person:

(a) By endorsement either to such person or in blank and by the transfer of possession of the negotiable cargo document to that person; or

(b) By mere transfer of possession of the negotiable cargo document to that person, if the last endorsement is in blank.

## CHAPTER 4. SPECIAL CONDITIONS FOR ELECTRONIC NEGOTIABLE CARGO DOCUMENTS

*Article 12. Requirements for an electronic negotiable cargo document*

1. A negotiable cargo document may be in the form of an electronic record provided that a reliable method is used:

(a) To identify that electronic record as the negotiable cargo document;

(b) To render that electronic record capable of being subject to control from its issuance until it ceases to have any effect or validity; and

(c) To retain the integrity of that electronic record.

2. The criterion for assessing integrity shall be whether information contained in the negotiable cargo document, including any authorized change that arises from its issuance until it ceases to have any effect or validity, has remained complete and unaltered apart from any change which arises in the normal course of communication, storage and display.

*Article 13. Content requirements*

For the purposes of this Convention, a requirement for information to be contained in a negotiable cargo document is met with respect to an electronic record if the information contained therein is accessible so as to be usable for subsequent reference.

*Article 14. Signature requirements*

For the purposes of this Convention, a requirement for a negotiable cargo document to be signed is met with respect to an electronic record if a reliable method is used to identify the signatory and to indicate that person's intention in respect of the information contained in the electronic record.

*Article 15. Possession requirements*

1. For the purposes of this Convention, a requirement for a negotiable cargo document to be possessed is met with respect to an electronic record if a reliable method is used:

(a) To establish exclusive control of that electronic record by a person; and

(b) To identify that person as the person in control.

2. A requirement to transfer possession of a negotiable cargo document is met with respect to an electronic record through the transfer of control over the electronic record.

*Article 16. Endorsement requirements*

For the purposes of this Convention, a requirement for a negotiable cargo document to be endorsed is met if the information required for the endorsement is included in the electronic record and that information is compliant with the requirements set forth in articles 13 and 14.

*Article 17. Change of medium*

1. If so agreed between the transport operator and the holder, the transport operator shall change the medium of the negotiable cargo document from a paper document to an electronic record or from an electronic record to a paper document provided that a reliable method for the change of medium is used.

2. For the change of medium to take effect:

(a) The holder shall surrender to the transport operator all originals of the negotiable cargo document in its previous medium; and

(b) The negotiable cargo document in its new medium shall include a statement that it replaces the negotiable cargo document in its previous medium.

3. Upon a change of medium, all originals of the negotiable cargo document in its previous medium shall be made inoperative and cease to have any effect or validity.

4. A change of medium in accordance with this article shall not affect the rights and obligations of the parties.

*Article 18. General reliability standard*

The method referred to in this chapter shall be:

(a) As reliable as appropriate for the fulfilment of the function for which the method is being used, in the light of all relevant circumstances, which may include:

(i) Any operational rules relevant to the assessment of reliability;

(ii) The assurance of data integrity;

(iii) The ability to prevent unauthorized access to and use of the system used to implement the method;

(iv) The security of hardware and software;

(v) The regularity and extent of audit by an independent body;

(vi) The existence of a declaration by a supervisory body, an accreditation body or a voluntary scheme regarding the reliability of the method;

(vii) Any applicable industry standard; or

(b) Proven in fact to have fulfilled the function by itself or together with further evidence.

# CHAPTER 5. FINAL CLAUSES

*Article 19. Depositary*

The Secretary-General of the United Nations is hereby designated as the depositary of this Convention.

*Article 20. Signature, ratification, acceptance, approval, accession*

1. This Convention is open for signature by all States.

2. This Convention is subject to ratification, acceptance or approval by the signatories.

3. This Convention is open for accession by all States that are not signatories as from the date it is open for signature.

4. Instruments of ratification, acceptance, approval or accession are to be deposited with the depositary.

*Article 21. Participation by regional economic integration organizations*

1. A regional economic integration organization that is constituted by States and has competence over certain matters governed by this Convention may similarly sign, ratify, accept, approve or accede to the Convention. The regional economic integration organization shall in that case have the rights and obligations of a State Party, to the extent that that organization has competence over matters governed by this Convention. For the purposes of articles 25 and 26, an instrument deposited by a regional economic integration organization shall not be counted in addition to the instruments deposited by its member States.

2. The regional economic integration organization shall make a declaration specifying the matters governed by this Convention in respect of which competence has been transferred to that organization by its member States. The regional economic integration organization shall promptly notify the depositary of any changes to the distribution of competence, including new transfers of competence, specified in the declaration made under this paragraph.

3. Any reference to a "State", "States", "State Party" or "States Parties" in this Convention applies equally to a regional economic integration organization where the context so requires.

*Article 22. Non-unified legal systems*

1. If a State has two or more territorial units in which different systems of law are applicable in relation to the matters dealt with in this Convention, it may declare that this Convention shall extend to all its territorial units or only to one or more of them.

2. Declarations made under this article shall state expressly the territorial units to which this Convention extends.

3. If a State makes a declaration under paragraph 1 that this Convention shall extend to one or more but not all its territorial units, a place located in a territorial unit to which this Convention does not extend is not considered to be in a State Party for the purposes of this Convention.

4. If a State makes no declaration under paragraph 1, this Convention shall extend to all territorial units of that State.

*Article 23. Procedure and effects of declarations*

1. Declarations under article 21, paragraph 2, and article 22, paragraph 1, shall be made at the time of signature, ratification, acceptance, approval or accession. Declarations made at the time of signature are subject to confirmation upon ratification, acceptance or approval.

2. Declarations and their confirmations shall be made in writing and formally notified to the depositary.

3. A declaration takes effect simultaneously with the entry into force of this Convention in respect of the State concerned.

4. Any State that makes a declaration under article 21, paragraph 2, and article 22, paragraph 1, may modify or withdraw it at any time by a formal notification in writing addressed to the depositary. The modification or withdrawal shall take effect 180 days after the date of the receipt of the notification by the depositary. If the depositary receives the notification of the modification or withdrawal before the entry into force of this Convention in respect of the State concerned, the modification or withdrawal shall take effect simultaneously with the entry into force of this Convention in respect of that State.

*Article 24. Reservations*

1. A State may declare, at the time of the deposit of its instrument of ratification, acceptance, approval or accession or at any time thereafter, that it will not apply this Convention to any negotiable transport document that evidences or contains a contract for the carriage of goods wholly by sea governed by an international convention to which it is a State Party.

2. Article 23, paragraphs 2 to 4, apply to reservations made under paragraph 1.

3. No reservations are permitted except as expressly authorized in this article.

*Article 25. Entry into force*

1. This Convention shall enter into force 180 days after the date of the deposit of the tenth instrument of ratification, acceptance, approval or accession.

2. When a State ratifies, accepts, approves or accedes to this Convention after the deposit of the tenth instrument of ratification, acceptance, approval or accession, this Convention shall enter into force in respect of that State 180 days after the date of the deposit of its instrument of ratification, acceptance, approval or accession.

*Article 26. Amendment*

1. Any State Party may propose an amendment to this Convention by submitting it to the Secretary-General of the United Nations. The Secretary-General shall

thereupon communicate the proposed amendment to the States Parties with a request that they indicate whether they favour a conference of States Parties for the purpose of considering and voting upon the proposal. In the event that within 120 days from the date of such communication at least one third of the States Parties favour such a conference, the Secretary-General shall convene the conference under the auspices of the United Nations.

2. The conference of States Parties shall make every effort to achieve consensus on each amendment. If all efforts at consensus are exhausted and no consensus is reached, the amendment shall, as a last resort, require for its adoption a two-thirds majority vote of the States Parties present and voting at the conference. For the purposes of this paragraph, the vote of a regional economic integration organization shall not be counted.

3. An adopted amendment shall be submitted by the depositary to all States Parties for ratification, acceptance or approval.

4. An adopted amendment shall enter into force 180 days after the date of deposit of the tenth instrument of ratification, acceptance or approval. When an amendment enters into force, it shall be binding on those States Parties that have expressed consent to be bound by it.

5. When a State Party ratifies, accepts or approves an amendment following the deposit of the tenth instrument of ratification, acceptance or approval, the amendment shall enter into force in respect of that State Party 180 days after the date of the deposit of its instrument of ratification, acceptance or approval.

*Article 27. Denunciation*

1. A State Party may denounce this Convention by a formal notification in writing addressed to the depositary. The denunciation may be limited to certain territorial units of a non-unified legal system to which this Convention applies.

2. The denunciation shall take effect 365 days after the date of the receipt of the notification by the depositary. Where a longer period for the denunciation to take effect is specified in the notification, the denunciation shall take effect upon the expiration of such longer period after the date of the receipt of the notification by the depositary.

DONE in a single original, of which the Arabic, Chinese, English, French, Russian and Spanish texts are equally authentic.

# Annex II

## List of documents before the Commission at its fifty-eighth session

| *Symbol* | *Title or description* |
|---|---|
| A/CN.9/1192 | Provisional agenda, annotations thereto and scheduling of meetings of the fifty-eighth session |
| A/CN.9/1193 | Report of Working Group II (Dispute Settlement) on the work of its eightieth session |
| A/CN.9/1194 | Report of Working Group III (Investor-State Dispute Settlement Reform) on the work of its forty-ninth session |
| A/CN.9/1195 | Report of Working Group III (Investor-State Dispute Settlement Reform) on the work of its fiftieth session |
| A/CN.9/1196 | Report of Working Group III (Investor-State Dispute Settlement Reform) on the work of its fifty-first session, first part |
| A/CN.9/1196/Add.1 | Report of Working Group III (Investor-State Dispute Settlement Reform) on the work of its fifty-first session, second part |
| A/CN.9/1197 | Report of Working Group IV (Electronic Commerce) on the work of its sixty-seventh session |
| A/CN.9/1198 | Report of Working Group V (Insolvency Law) on the work of its sixty-fifth session |
| A/CN.9/1199 | Report of Working Group VI (Negotiable Cargo Documents) on the work of its forty-fifth session |
| A/CN.9/1200 | Report of Working Group II (Dispute Settlement) on the work of its eighty-first session |
| A/CN.9/1201 | Report of the Colloquium on Secured Transactions |
| A/CN.9/1202 | Report of Working Group IV (Electronic Commerce) on the work of its sixty-eighth session |
| A/CN.9/1203 | Report of Working Group V (Insolvency Law) on the work of its sixty-sixth session |
| A/CN.9/1204 | Report of the Colloquium on the Law of International Trade for a Greener Future |
| A/CN.9/1205 | Report of Working Group VI (Negotiable Cargo Documents) on the work of its forty-sixth session |
| A/CN.9/1206 | Bibliography of recent writings related to the work of UNCITRAL |
| A/CN.9/1207 | Status of conventions and model laws and other UNCITRAL texts |
| A/CN.9/1208 | Relevant General Assembly resolutions |
| A/CN.9/1209 | Non-legislative activities |
| A/CN.9/1209/Add.1 | Non-legislative activities – Technical cooperation and assistance |
| A/CN.9/1209/Add.2 | Non-legislative activities – Activities of the UNCITRAL Regional Centre for Asia and the Pacific |
| A/CN.9/1209/Add.3 | Non-legislative activities – Ways and means of ensuring a uniform interpretation and application of international conventions and uniform laws in the field of the law of international trade: CLOUT, digests and other materials |

| *Symbol* | *Title or description* |
|---|---|
| A/CN.9/1209/Add.4 | Non-legislative activities – Transparency repository |
| A/CN.9/1209/Add.5 | Non-legislative activities – The online and social media presence of UNCITRAL |
| A/CN.9/1209/Add.6 | Non-legislative activities – UNCITRAL Law Library, publications, press releases and other outreach activities |
| A/CN.9/1209/Add.7 | Non-legislative activities – UNCITRAL internship programme and co-sponsored moots |
| A/CN.9/1209/Add.8 | Non-legislative activities – Planned activities in the second half of 2025 |
| A/CN.9/1209/Add.9 | Non-legislative activities – Resources and funding |
| A/CN.9/1210 | Work programme of the Commission |
| A/CN.9/1211 | Coordination activities |
| A/CN.9/1212 | Coordination and cooperation – International governmental and non-governmental organizations invited to sessions of UNCITRAL and its working groups |
| A/CN.9/1213 | Draft convention on negotiable cargo documents |
| A/CN.9/1214 | Compilation of comments on the draft convention on negotiable cargo documents |
| A/CN.9/1214/Add.1 | Compilation of comments on the draft convention on negotiable cargo documents |
| A/CN.9/1215 | Stocktaking of developments in dispute resolution in the digital economy – progress report |
| A/CN.9/1216 | Compilation of comments on the UNCITRAL-UNIDROIT study on the legal nature of verified carbon credits issued by independent carbon standard setters |
| A/CN.9/1216/Add.1 | Compilation of comments on the UNCITRAL-UNIDROIT study on the legal nature of verified carbon credits issued by independent carbon standard setters |
| A/CN.9/1216/Add.2 | Additional comments on the UNCITRAL-UNIDROIT study on the legal nature of verified carbon credits issued by independent carbon standard setters |
| A/CN.9/1216/Add.3 | Additional comments on the UNCITRAL-UNIDROIT study on the legal nature of verified carbon credits issued by independent carbon standard setters |
| A/CN.9/1217 | Resources to implement the work programme with respect to investor-State dispute settlement reform |
| A/CN.9/1218 | Summary of the second meeting on the operationalization of the Advisory Centre on International Investment Dispute Resolution |
| A/CN.9/1219 | Possible future work in the area of insolvency law |
| A/CN.9/1220 | Possible reform of investor-State dispute settlement – draft toolkit on prevention and mitigation of international investment disputes |
| A/CN.9/1221 | Compilation of comments on the draft texts on asset tracing and recovery in insolvency proceedings |
| A/CN.9/1221/Add.1 | Compilation of comments on the draft texts on asset tracing and recovery in insolvency proceedings |

| *Symbol* | *Title or description* |
| --- | --- |
| A/CN.9/1222 | Draft guidance document on legal issues relating to the use of distributed ledger technology in trade |
| A/CN.9/1223 | Role of UNCITRAL in promoting the rule of law at the national and international levels |
| A/CN.9/1224 | Submission from the Inclusive Global Legal Innovation Platform on Online Dispute Resolution |
| A/CN.9/1225 | Legal issues relating to the use of decentralized autonomous organizations in trade |
| A/CN.9/1226 | Stocktaking of UNCITRAL texts referring to electronic aspects |
| A/CN.9/1227 | Proposal by the United Arab Emirates and Spain on possible future work on legal aspects of digital trade |
| A/CN.9/1228 | Draft model organization rules |
| A/CN.9/1229 | Possible future work in the area of digital payments |
| A/CN.9/1230 | Possible future work in the area of public procurement |
| A/CN.9/1231 | Proposal by Viet Nam for possible future work on carbon markets |
| A/CN.9/1232 | Submission by the Government of France for future work on insolvency, the environment and sustainability |
| A/CN.9/1233 | Submission by the Government of Israel regarding exploratory work on remote arbitration and mediation |
| A/CN.9/1234 | Proposal by the Russian Federation on possible future work on legal aspects of paperless trade |